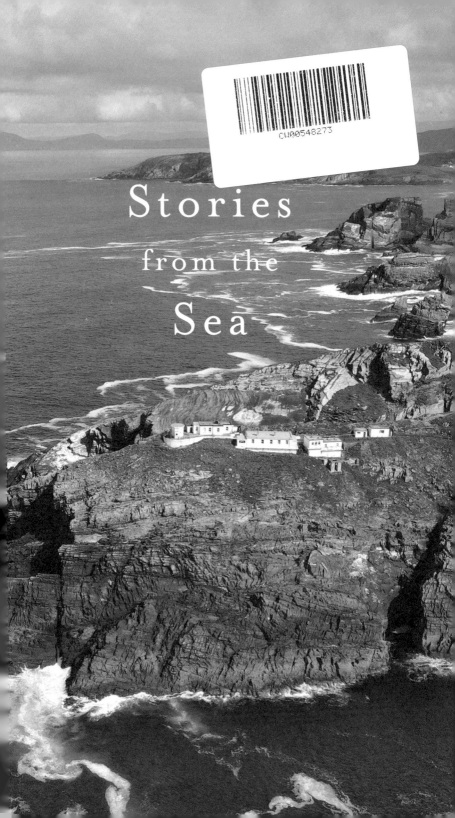

Stories
from the
Sea

First published 2021 by The O'Brien Press Ltd.,
12 Terenure Road East, Rathgar, Dublin 6, D06 HD27, Ireland.
Tel: +353 1 4923333; Fax: +353 1 4922777
E-mail: books@obrien.ie. Website: www.obrien.ie
The O'Brien Press is a member of Publishing Ireland.

ISBN: 978-1-78849-205-8

10 9 8 7 6 5 4 3 2 1
25 24 23 22 21

Photography by Richard Mills

Printed and bound in Drukarnia Skleniarz, Poland.
The paper in this book is produced using pulp from managed forests.

Published in
DUBLIN
UNESCO
City of Literature

Stories

from the

Sea

Legends, adventures and tragedies
of Ireland's coast

Jo Kerrigan & Richard Mills

THE O'BRIEN PRESS
DUBLIN

JO KERRIGAN was born and bred in Cork, where she took her first two degrees at UCC before moving to the UK to continue her academic work. After a distinguished career there, including winning the Oxbow Prize for medieval history at Oxford, she returned to her roots to apply her research skills to Ireland's undiscovered past. A specialist in ancient crafts and folklore, she now devotes herself to exploring how everyday life was lived long ago.

RICHARD MILLS was born in Provence, and moved to Ireland at the age of sixteen. His long and successful career as a press photographer was combined with a passion for wildlife, and his pictures have garnered numerous national and international awards. He was the subject of a TV programme by the wildlife film-maker Éamon de Buitléar, and he has contributed images to hundreds of publications across the world, as well as his own popular book, *Ireland's Bird Life: A World of Beauty*.

Jo and Richard live in West Cork, surrounded by books and cameras, cats and dogs. Previous books for O'Brien Press include *West Cork: A Place Apart*; *Old Ways, Old Secrets*; and *Follow the Old Road*.

This book is dedicated to all those who, over
thousands of years, have sailed to and from Ireland.

Contents

The Cailleach or Hag of Beara, an echo of our ancient past.

Introduction

As a small island nation, ours is a culture inextricably bound up with the seas that surround us. From earliest times, travellers in fragile craft from far-off lands have crossed the oceans to our shores, seeking a place to settle or to trade the goods they carried. Later, others came with plunder in mind, seizing the rich bounty that this fertile soil produces so effortlessly.

Over millennia, our people have earned their livings from the waters that lap our shores. They have built small boats and huge ships, the better to traverse those surrounding waters. They have learned to read the skies and sense the changing of the wind. In stormy weather, many a vessel has come to grief on the hungry rocks that are always waiting for new victims, while in secret inlets on calm, moonless nights, bales and barrels have been swiftly unloaded and spirited away to safe hiding places.

A vital source of nourishment, a natural means of travel, a source of food and income; friendly and smiling or threatening and deadly, the sea has influenced Ireland and its people since the beginning. It has brought goods, ideas, invaders, influences, and taken away emigrants, pilgrims, evangelising monks, adventurers. All have played their part in our history.

Here, then, are just some of the salt-drenched stories that have come from Ireland's endless involvement with its surrounding waters. Age-old legends of fantastic voyages and strange demonic invaders; thrilling tales of storms, shipwrecks and smuggling; stirring accounts of little coastal traders and huge transatlantic liners; exciting ideas from those who pushed the boundaries of communication. Read them, feel the tug of the sea breeze in your hair, get the scent of the brine, and feel you are there.

The Sea
Carried Them

THE LEGENDARY FIRST SETTLERS
TO IRELAND

People have been drawn to Ireland, with her gentle climate and fertile soil, for millennia; ever since the withdrawal of the Ice Age, in fact. The *Lebor Gabála Érenn*, or *Book of Invasions*, is a collection of poems and prose chronicling the multiple waves of settlers who sought this green island on the westernmost edge of what was then the known world. The collection was first committed to writing by Christian scribes around the eleventh century, but the text is firmly based in oral tradition going back into prehistory, handed down from father to son, generation to generation, storyteller to storyteller.

'This is how it happened and how we came to be what we are today, these are the people who came to Ireland long long ago ...' the shanachie would softly chant to a spellbound audience.

Naturally enough, every single one of these early settlers used the sea as their high road to Ireland. Some may not even have intended to come here: they might have been swept before a storm or missed their planned destination in fog; they may not have had an idea of where on the great ocean they actually were. In ancient times, you quite often ended up where Aeolus, god of the winds, felt like sending you – if your cargo or mission was to somewhere very different, well, that was your problem and you had to make the best of it.

Whether the waves of settlers chronicled in the *Lebor Gabála* came by accident or intention, they travelled here across the ocean. Most came with the prevailing trade winds from the southeast, from Asia, Greece, Sicily, Spain; but some at least came from the colder Northlands, and one group indeed (if the legends are to be believed) from a threatening and grim Undersea world.

Of course, there is a great deal of embroidery and expansion in these old legends, but at the heart of every such tale is a germ of truth, a shred of folk memory going back generations, an enshrining of actual facts and happenings, around which the story has been developed. However fanciful they may appear, they are still telling us something about the far distant past, and should be valued as such. Here, then, are some of the legendary stories of those who came by sea.

Cessair

According to the *Book of Invasions*, the very first traveller to reach Ireland was Cessair, who came from far in the south-east, escaping from the Great Flood. Christian scribes copying down the tale according to their standards identify her firmly as Noah's granddaughter, but that was probably what one might call monkish licence, slotting her into an acceptable Biblical context. Whatever her origins, she was definitely a woman, not the usual armed warrior of legend, and she landed on the Dingle Peninsula in Kerry:

> *This is the reason for her coming, fleeing from the*
> *Flood: for Noe said unto them: Rise, said he* [and go]
> *to the western edge of the world; perchance the Flood*
> *may not reach it. The crew of three ships arrived at*
> *Dun na mRarc in the territory of Corco Daibne.*

The Flood or Deluge isn't really our concern here, but it is fascinating to ponder on what it might actually have been, what its causes were, how large an area was affected. In our own time, we have seen disastrous tsunamis caused by volcanic eruptions and earthquakes, and it could well be that a similar natural disaster is echoed, however vaguely, in the Biblical stories of Noah and his Ark.

Modern research inclines toward the theory that the Flood was caused by the original barrier between the Mediterranean and the Black Sea (then a freshwater lake) breaking, loosing vast amounts of water from the former to the latter. This may have been caused by a tsunami or by rising temperatures after the Ice Age. Certainly, recent deep-water explorations of the Black Sea coast have revealed an original shoreline and ancient shipwrecks, hundreds of metres below present-day sea level. (Mount Ararat, where the Ark finds its final resting place in the story, is in eastern Turkey, which would add strength to this idea.)

After the first deadly rush, the waters would have continued to rise steadily, and survivors would have had to either move further and further up into the hills or take to boats and seek new lands.

Cessair, according to legend, was able to organise a fleet of ships and a strong band of female followers for this migration, so she was clearly somebody of importance. In fact, she is likely to have been a seer or high priestess, perhaps from Egypt, and certainly somebody possessing both strength and power, which would explain why the monks were so quick to ascribe to her a Biblical parentage. Most emphatically, it would *not* do to have strange women from distinctly unacceptable religious backgrounds taking the principal role in the start of Ireland's history.

Cessair's journey from the east was not an easy one, encountering fierce storms and high winds that sank two of their craft and drowned many of the travellers, both the women and their armed male escort. (That male escort is another indication of the leader's social importance.) It is one of the first records of stormy weather and shipwreck, themes that are to recur again and again in stories from the sea down through the centuries.

Wild waves threatened those trying to reach Ireland.

Cessair herself survived, along with fifty women and just three men. Making sensible plans for their future in Ireland, she divided her female followers into three groups, each under the protection of one of the men, and she herself married Fintan, the bravest and strongest of these.

However, after some time, these fortunate (or unfortunate, depending how you look at it) men eventually died, and the practical Cessair realised that she had only one man, her husband Fintan, to ensure the future of the settlement. Giving a very human twist to the legend, he realised that he could not possibly satisfy fifty women. He lost heart and fled into the wilderness. The abandoned Cessair died of a broken heart, and her abandoned followers too eventually died out.

Fintan, somewhere out there in the wild, was the only one left of those first arrivals. He must have learned some of his wife's magical skills, as he managed to survive down through the ages by being reborn as many different creatures: a salmon, an eagle, a boar, a hawk and more. He lived for 5,000 years, so that he could recount to later settlers the history of Ireland as he had seen it since the beginning.

One variation of the legend says that the Great Flood eventually reached Ireland and only Fintan survived, by changing himself into a salmon in a submerged cave known afterwards as Fintan's Grave. This cave is said to be hidden on the mountain called *Tul Tuinde*, or Hill of the Wave, near Lough Derg on the Shannon.

Fintan survived by changing himself into a salmon, and then an eagle.

Parthalon

After Cessair, it is said, Ireland lay empty until the coming of Parthalon, who came all the way from Greece, via Sicily, in a sea journey that took two and a half months. He and his people are said by some to have landed near Kenmare in Kerry.

> *Now Ireland was waste [thereafter], for a space of three hundred years, till Parthalon came to it. He is the first who took Ireland after the Flood, on a Tuesday, on the fourteenth of the moon, in Inber Scene: [for three times was Ireland taken in Inber Scene].*

Henry Morris, in a detailed lecture given to the Royal Society of Antiquaries in 1937, maintains that Parthalon landed not in Kerry but at the mouth of the Erne in Donegal, where the town of Ballyshannon stands today.

Parthalon settled on an island in the River Erne.

Parthalon settled on an island here with his wife Delgnat and his followers, making their living by fishing in the rich waters of the river. One day, so the legend relates, he went off to fish, leaving Delgnat in the care of one of his servants. Clearly this servant must have been attractive, since the lord of the island came home to find them having rather too fond a time together. Furious, he turned on his wife's pet dog, which came leaping to greet him, and killed it with a blow. This would in fact have been a major offence in ancient Ireland, under Brehon law, and would have been perceived as such by listeners to the tale.

Delgnat, however, gave as good as she got, asking Parthalon what else he expected if he were to leave her alone all day with temptation laid out in front of her. It's an observant touch, and notable that it is dutifully recorded in the old text, even though written down by Christian scribes. Women in those times had minds of their own, unlike the obedient and sub-servient wives of later literature. The event was ever afterwards claimed to be the first instance of jealousy in Ireland (and also, incidentally, the first of adultery).

Parthalon, and his descendants after him, lived many years in Ireland (300, according to the *Lebor Gabála*), and cleared much of the heavy woodland that covered that part of the northwest in which they settled, in order to graze cattle and plant crops. He is in fact credited with being the first to intro-duce cattle, to till the land, to churn butter and to brew ale. Clearly a man of practical sense and skill was Parthalon.

Once again, these are indications that the legend is based on real events of the far distant past. If it wasn't precisely

Parthalon and his followers, somebody certainly came, stayed and cleared woodland. Those are the basic facts that are remembered over the generations.

In the end though, according to the *Lebor Gabála*, the entire Parthalon tribe died in a single week of a dreadful sickness. This was in all probability the 'yellow plague', which is recorded in old sources as recurring regularly. That could have been bubonic plague, better known in medieval times as the Black Death, or perhaps smallpox. One might think, given the descriptive 'yellow', that it was a form of jaundice, but that couldn't really be described as a virulent and fatal disease. Bubonic plague, on the other hand, is spread by fleas, carried by rats, and there would have been plenty of both around in ancient times.

Whatever the identity of the swift-moving pandemic, it is held to have wiped out the Parthalonians within the space of seven days. For a long time, it was held that this happened on the site of modern-day Tallaght (*Tamleacht*, the Plain of the Plague), just southwest of Dublin, but more recently there have been disputes about the location. *Tamleacht* is a name found all over Ireland, in places where many have died at one time of an epidemic, and several of these are nearer to where Parthalon is said to have lived on the west coast.

After that, Ireland remained empty and silent for thirty years, say the legends. Perhaps there was no-one left after the plague to go adventuring on the sea; perhaps the fear of the infection kept new invaders away.

It was thirty lean years that she
was empty in the face of war-champions,
after the death of her host throughout a week

Nemed

But then came Nemed and his followers, from the land of Scythia, far away on the very borders of Europe and Asia. The Scythians were a group of ancient tribes, mainly nomads, who came originally from Siberia and spread gradually outwards as far as the Black Sea. The name Nemed means 'holy' or 'privileged' in ancient Irish, and this new invader may well have been a druid – or, given that they came originally from Siberia, a shaman.

He and his tribe set sail from the Caspian Sea in forty-four ships, but only one survived to reach the Irish shore, after storms and catastrophes. One such disaster came about when the voyagers saw a golden tower floating in the sea and tried to conquer it. As a result, many of the boats were wrecked. An allegory or a real-life iceberg? One wouldn't expect an iceberg along the complex route they must have taken from the Caspian Sea. Up into the Volga River and then down the Don into the Sea of Azov and on to the Black Sea, through the Bosphorus (if there was a way through, otherwise a bit of overland portaging would have been necessary) and into the Aegean. Then along the Mediterranean, around Iberia (modern Spain and Portugal), up past what is now France and across to Ireland. Nevertheless, it is an interesting echo of those iceberg encounters which occur in the ancient *imramma* or travel tales (see later sections of this chapter).

Nemed landed at Great Island in Cork Harbour.

The Nemedians landed at Great Island in Cork Harbour, on Ireland's south coast. In old Irish, Great Island was known as *Oileán Ard Neimheadh*.

Puzzlingly, though, we are told that Nemed's wife died twelve days after their arrival, and was buried at Ard Macha or Armagh, which lies almost 400km to the north. Geographically, that isn't really possible. But then, it was common for storytellers to ascribe a particular location to an important event when it seemed politic so to do. That is, if you are being housed and feasted in a noble hall or indeed a monastery or abbey in the north of the country, you would naturally emphasise the importance of local places in your tale.

A more practical solution to this puzzle of location lies in the woman's name. Since she was called Macha, it is likely that the hill or cairn where her body was entombed would have been christened Ard Macha, wherever it was located. Irish place names, in both their original and their present-day forms, are a challenging study all on their own.

After only nine years, Nemed and 3,000 of his followers also died of that endemic plague. He himself is said to have been buried on Great Island, where he first landed. The few who survived the infection were, naturally enough, somewhat less than enamoured with Ireland, and decided on emigration – but in three groups. Two retraced their sea-steps to Greece, while the third moved sideways to the neighbouring island of Britain, which had a very similar landscape and climate to Ireland.

The Fir Bolg and the Tuatha Dé Danaan

That section of the Nemedians who crossed to Britain decided to stay on, and thus became the ancestors of all future Britons. Those who went back to Greece, though, eventually returned to Ireland. One group had fared badly by landing among tribes where wealthy aristocrats enslaved the poorer people; thus these luckless survivors became slaves themselves. They are said to have been forced to work at gathering rich soil and carrying it to poorer land to improve crops, using large leather bags to do so. One imagines them longingly telling their children stories of the green land far to the northwest where crops grew almost by themselves, so fertile was the soil.

Eventually their descendants managed to escape, using those very leather bags to construct boats, and they journeyed northwest across the oceans to find this wonderful place. Later generations were to christen them the Fir Bolg, or Bag Men, on account of this. When they reached Ireland, they set about tilling the land and enjoying a free life at last. Not for long, though.

The descendants of the second group that had gone south were quite different in outlook. The Greece of ancient times stretched far in many directions, and it would seem that they had settled in the Near East, where wise men studied ancient arts. Here they learned the complex skills of druidism, philosophy and even magic. A couple of centuries later, they returned to Ireland, this time as the Tuatha Dé Danaan.

Of course, it may not have happened exactly this way. The remnants of one tribe abandoned this island; much later, other groups came. There may not have been any connection at all. The *Book of Invasions* is adamant though that those who left as Nemedians came back as either the Fir Bolg or the Tuatha Dé Danaan. As is always the case, there is very likely to be a germ of historical truth buried somewhere in there.

All the old sources agree though that the age of the Tuatha Dé Danaan was a golden one, an era of beauty and joy, music and song. Tall, golden-haired and powerful in magic, after defeating the Fir Bolg in battle, the Tuatha Dé Danaan did not

Lazy beds on Inisheer, Aran Islands.

drive them out entirely, but pushed them across to the western coast and its islands. Were the Fir Bolg then the ancestors of those who put to sea even today in lightweight currachs, and collect soil from the mainland to make 'lazy beds' for growing crops on the harsh and rocky Aran Islands?

So far, the legend of these settlers may read as a fairly peaceful sequence of events over centuries, even allowing for the inevitable battles for supremacy among waves of invaders. But a particular group, of a very different and more frightening nature, which threatened, attacked and oppressed all of these groups of settlers one after another, has been impatiently waiting its turn to come into the foreground. It has been kept out of the story until now, because if ever a tribe deserved full individual attention, it is this one.

Came from beneath the sea? The Fomorians

Who exactly were the Fomorians? Legends speak of them with fear and horror. The earliest tales describe them as monstrous creatures who came not *over* the sea but from *under* it, bringing terror to those dwelling peacefully on land. One-eyed and one-legged are included in their legendary attributes, but the abiding theme is of brutality, oppression, extortion. No question here of living in peaceful harmony, sharing the fruits of labour. The Fomorians descended in hordes from the ocean, attacking any settlement and demanding taxes in food, slaves and even children. Naturally enough, in later times, their story became blended with that of Viking raiders, but the originals were quite terrifying enough without any additions.

Sea pirates certainly, but from where? Perhaps they were early Norsemen, but their physical difference to the land-based settlers of Ireland is always emphasised. Grotesque, dark-skinned, terrifying, seeking only to attack and seize, they were feared everywhere along the coast. And they did not scruple to join in battle when desperate groups of settlers tried to oppose their demands. Nemed's people fought them, as did Parthalon's, and the Tuatha Dé Danaan, the last finally managing to drive them from our shores.

Tradition has long held that their main outpost close to the Irish mainland was on Tory Island off Donegal, using as the main justification of their argument the ancient name of Balor's island, *Tor Inis*, but a study by Henry Morris in the 1930s makes a very convincing argument for Dernish Island, just off the Sligo shore.

Derinish Island – was this the home of Balor?

As part of his argument, he quotes the original text, which describes how the Nemedians, in one battle, attacked the Fomorians both by land and by sea. This would not make sense if Tory Island was the stronghold of the enemy, since it is already almost 15km (9 miles) off the Donegal coast.

Further, there is a very descriptive passage detailing how the forces are so engaged in fighting on the strand that they do not notice the tide rising around them, and eventually they are all drowned. This again doesn't fit Tory's rocky shoreline, but works very well into the geographical layout at Dernish – here there is a wide sandbank that is exposed at low water but covered at full tide, and the tide turns notoriously quickly.

How were the Fomorians so successful in their raids and their demands? What gave them the superior strength that enabled them to oppress so many tribes over such a long period?

Tory Island.

Cattle still cross to Derinish at low tide, just as the Nemedians did so long ago.

Well, now we come to perhaps the most feared of all old Irish figures, one used by countless parents over the millennia to threaten their children into good behaviour. The Fomorians had a secret power – almost, you might say, a weapon of mass destruction – that they could unleash to wreak havoc on the strongest band of opposing warriors.

Balor of the Evil Eye

The Fomorians were malevolent and demonic, both in their looks and in their warlike ways, but Balor was feared most of all. Our legends are full of frightening stories about his dreadful appearance, most of all because of that one terrifying and fatal eye in the middle of his forehead. He had only to look on an opposing army for every one of them to fall dead. Because of this, some tales say, his eye was normally bandaged, and he was led by two of his followers until the moment came to remove the bandage and let the terror loose on the enemy. Other versions say there was a brass ring in his eyelid and it took seven men to lift it. Other tales describe seven separate layers of leather hiding it from view (seven being one of the magical numbers).

Aodh de Blacam, in his thrilling tale *The Druid's Cave* (1920), transposes two young men of the present day back to that ancient time, where they lend their field glasses to King Conall so that he can see the dreaded figure approaching in the far distance:

> *'Tis Balor himself; who would not know that evil form? Balor the death-dealer; Balor whose deadly eye can slay man by its gaze even at a league's distance! Balor is not dead: he has escaped, he lives, he is back!*

King Conaill sees the dreaded Balor through modern field glasses.

Eventually, according to one source, Balor was slain by Lugh of the Tuatha Dé Danann, who was in fact his daughter's son, thereby fulfilling the prophecy that the monster would die at his own grandson's hands. Lugh fired a slingshot with deadly accuracy right through that fatal eye, thrusting it back into the fiend's head. Another tale, slightly later in date, says Balor survived the injury and was chased by Lugh all the way to the southernmost tip of Ireland at Mizen Head. Here he was killed, and his head was set on a large rock, which immediately shattered, forming his cairn.

There is more than an echo of both the Cyclops and Medusa in the tales of Balor, but that isn't surprising, given the apparently regular journeys made between Ireland and Greece by these settlers. But who were the Fomorians, and did they really exist?

Early legends say they were monsters who came from beneath the sea itself; later versions describe them as sea raiders who used offshore islands as their bases and came ashore to harry those dwelling on the mainland. Given that the later Vikings were also in the habit of using offshore or estuarine islands as bases, they might well have been early Norsemen. Or, given the many descriptions of their dark skin and monstrous appearance, is there some other, more eerie explanation?

Still: Balor slain; the Fomorians driven back to sea. Now could the Tuatha Dé Danann settle down in peace and quiet? Alas, no. Yet another invader was already preparing to cross the sea to Ireland.

The Coming of the Celts

The Milesians, later known as the Celts, had been moving inexorably westward across Europe for many thousands of years. It is said that they had long believed their destiny lay in green Inisfáil, the island on the edge of the world. (Again and again, we are reminded that people long ago, in far-off lands, already knew of Ireland and its desirability, and knew how to get there.)

The Celts were a warlike people, ready to fight for what they wanted, and as they made their final voyage from Galicia in northern Spain, they were fully prepared for battle. Landing in Kerry, they stormed to the court of the Tuatha Dé Danann and demanded submission. Those skilful diplomats claimed reprovingly that they had been given no warning, no time for preparation. Go back to sea, they said, beyond the ninth wave, and give us time for fair fight.

The Celts agreed and returned to their boats, sailing out well beyond the ninth wave. In Irish tradition, this is the all-important dividing point beyond which the laws of the land do not run. Offenders were often sent beyond the ninth wave for their crimes, in a boat without oars, so that the sea could decide what to do with them. In the case of the invading Celts though, the Tuatha Dé Danaan knew just what to do.

'Let us trust to the powers,' said the druids, 'that they may never reach Ireland.' With that the druids cast druidic winds after them, so that the bottom gravel was raised to the top of the sea, so great was the storm;

Storms and mist were used by the Tuatha de Danaan to prevent the Celts landing.

so that the storm took them westward in the ocean
till they were weary. 'A druids' wind is that,' said
Donn, son of Mil. 'It is indeed,' said Amergin, 'unless
it be higher than the mast; find out for us if it be so.'
Erannan, the youngest son of Mil, went up the mast,
and said that it was not over them.

Confirming that it was indeed a magic mist, Amergin, himself a wise and learned druid, chanted a countering spell, which calmed the storm at once. And so the Celts came to Ireland to stay. The *Book of Invasions* claims that they then defeated the Tuatha Dé Danann in battle and drove them into the sea.

However, local tradition refutes that, insisting instead that these magical, bright-haired people used their skills to disappear into the hills, making their home forever after in the Otherworld, from where they could still watch their beloved country.

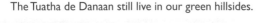

The Tuatha de Danaan still live in our green hillsides.

At certain times of year, it is still believed, they emerge and move around the upper world. They sometimes let themselves be seen, and often tempt unsuspecting young men and women to come away with them to Tír na nÓg, as Niamh of the Golden Hair did to Oisín, son of Finn McCool. On other occasions, a young Otherworld god might seduce a girl in the everyday world, who would then bring forth a stunningly beautiful and powerful warrior son, thus ensuring that the Tuatha Dé Danann genes would never quite die out. That was most likely to happen at the great summer and winter festivals of Bealtaine and Samhain, when the veil between this and the Otherworld is at its thinnest.

The coming of the Celts bridges the gap between legend and actual history, moving from a druidic world to a sternly factual one. From now on, invaders and raiders would be very real indeed. Well, except perhaps for one curious little group of settlers on the Cork/Kerry coast, who straddle the divide between tale and truth, remaining a mystery to this day.

The Ranties

You won't hear much about this strange community except in a throwaway remark by a local – 'Aren't you a right Rantie?' Even then, you might not find out much more than that a belligerent little tribe known as the Ranties are said to have lived in Kerry at one time. The historian Richard Caulfield did some research on the topic in the 1870s, establishing that these people had lived on Sugarloaf Mountain near Bantry, close to the border between

Cork and Kerry, in the previous century, keeping very much to themselves.

> *On the eastern slope of this mountain, where the land borders on the sea, a curious race of people formerly dwelt, called 'Ranties.' A little before the close of the eighteenth century they possessed all the characteristics of a peculiar people ...*

In appearance they were very small indeed, apparently no more than four feet high. Caulfield attributes this to their determination to remain secretive and independent, marrying only among themselves and having as little to do with the outside world as possible. The language they spoke seems to have been some form of Irish, but was very difficult to understand.

The Ranties kept cows and goats, and lived principally on potatoes and fish. At certain times of the year, they would bring coral sand and seaweed to Bantry to sell to farmers for enriching the fields. Sailing small boats skilfully, they would bring their loads in on the full tide, hastening back to their mountain domain as soon as business had been transacted. It seems that they were a primitive maritime tribe who had followed the coastline and settled in this part of the country in ancient times because it suited their preferences, being wild and remote, and lacking roads.

One distinctive characteristic of the Rantie women was their habit of wearing red cloaks. The dye for these bright garments was obtained from shellfish by a secret method, jealously guarded (much like the 'Tyrian purple' of ancient Phoenicia). These cloaks may have been similar to the traditional Kerry cloak, with its many pleats and capacious hood, but, given the extravagant use of fabric in that design, those of the Rantie women may have been more economical in cut.

A local legend states that when the French fleet was threatening to invade in 1796, Lord Bantry ordered all of these women to assemble on the side of Sugarloaf to give the effect of many English redcoat soldiers, but this is unlikely to be true. Given their shyness, and their near-obsessive desire to avoid contact with other communities, the chances of their being, first of all, located, and second, persuaded to undertake such a task, are extremely slim. It's a nice image though.

A severe epidemic of cholera in 1832, followed some years later by the Famine, in all likelihood spelled the end of the Ranties and their mountainside community. Those who survived went on to intermarry with neighbouring communities and, probably reluctantly, adopt a more modern way of life.

There is an ancient burial place at Tracashel, called Killeenah, which is held to be the last resting place of the Ranties.

Those who had any contact with this strange community in the eighteenth century said that the Ranties themselves believed they had come from 'the North', but whether that meant Ulster or further north again – across the sea in the Hebrides, Shetland, the Faroes – was never made clear. Perhaps they didn't know themselves.

One knowledgeable Irish scholar at the time of Caulfield's research claimed that they came originally from Ulster around the sixteenth century, and were by nature and inclination robbers and plunderers, who chose a remote region on the coast as somewhere they were not easily to be discovered or apprehended. Another diligent researcher claimed that there was a similar race of people living at a place called Togher Rann, near Lahinch on the Clare coast. There is also a townland known as Ranafast in the Rosses in Donegal, again on the sea coast. It is appropriate to remember that 'Rann' was the Norse sea-god. Did the Ranties originally come from Norway? Could they possibly have had any connection to the dreaded Fomorians?

FANTASTIC VOYAGES

The *imramma* and *echtrae*, or magical voyage tales, passed down from generation to generation of storytellers, open up an enthralling world of mysterious islands beyond the horizon, terrifying monsters and evil giants, but also of generous, welcoming communities, wonderful creatures and rich landscapes with splendid flowers and bountiful fruit.

They were, in fact, the far precursor of both modern-day fantasy films, in which bewildered travellers encounter frightening worlds, with a wealth of special effects to keep the viewer gripped, and scenic travelogues, giving us vivid glimpses of nature's wonders. Mysterious islands with strange inhabitants and grotesque monsters – sounds familiar, doesn't it? Yet listeners in the wooden halls of old Irish kings, clustered round the fire and hanging on every word uttered by a visiting bard, knew that thrilling shiver up the spine just as well as anybody watching late-night movies now, and avid fans of David Attenborough's wildlife programmes had ancestors who also loved hearing of fascinating, far-flung places and exotic creatures.

To read through these ancient tales is to realise what a surprising knowledge of the wider world our ancestors actually possessed. Where and how this knowledge was gathered – whether it came from real voyages, from the legends of other cultures, or from the tall tales of visiting seamen – will never be fully established. These travelogues are most likely a combination of our own ancient legends (an *ollamh* or senior poet had to possess a treasure house in his head of 'seven times fifty stories'), tales told by traders from far-off countries, folk memories of those who originally came to Ireland from distant lands and, inevitably, quite a bit of adjustment by monks to make it more palatable for Christianised consumption. All could be, and were, blended together into wonderful evenings of storytelling.

That is the most important thing to remember: that originally these travel tales were recounted by the poet or shanachie by the fireside on winter nights to awestruck audiences, some-times being spun out over several evenings to lengthen the poet's stay under a comfortable, sheltering roof. They were passed down from one generation of storytellers to the next as a priceless oral heritage. Only with the arrival of Christianity and its lettered monks were they recorded in writing for the first time.

The Church would certainly not have missed the opportu-nity to remove references considered morally questionable, to alter the tenor of passages to reflect their new religious teaching and, where possible, to attribute all the miracles to one of their newly created saints rather than to an ancient hero. This is, after all, one tactic of an evangelising church. To get the full effect, such stories should always be heard, not read. Like all old Irish legends, the effect is created by the dramatic voice.

In modern academic circles, *imramma* are held to be the Christianised tales and *echtrae* the earlier, pagan ones. You can't make a strict division though, as most of the surviving tales (and alas, we have lost so many) include characteristics of both. It's not a vital distinction – what is important is that we still possess the earliest adventure stories and travelogues, introducing their hearers to wonders of the natural world and the habits and customs of other lands, whether real or imaginary. Today we watch the National Geographic chan-nel; our far ancestors had the *imramma* and *echtrae*, with all their surprises, dangers and thrills. An evening when the sto-ryteller agreed to recount one was a golden event indeed, to be remembered and talked over for years afterwards.

The Voyage of Bran MacFebal

This *immram* starts in true storytelling style with a mysterious woman appearing in the hall of the king and singing a song of temptation to Bran about the wonderful world beyond the horizon.

> *There are thrice fifty distant isles*
> *In the ocean to the west of us;*
> *Larger than Erin twice*
> *Is each of them, or thrice.*

Bran, consumed with desire to see the wonders of which she has sung, collects a band of followers (three companies of nine, observing the mystical rules) and sets off into the wide blue yonder. They meet Mananaan mac Lir, god of the sea, who describes the beauties of the land beneath the waves, unseen by human eyes. They reach the Island of Joy, where all the inhabitants are laughing senselessly, and the Island of Women, where they are treated as honoured guests with every comfort and attention.

Eventually though, as time slips by, Bran decides to turn for home, although the women warn him that none of them should try to land in Ireland.

> *Then they went until they arrived at a gathering at Srub*
> *Brain. The men asked of them who it was came over the*
> *sea. Said Bran: 'I am Bran the son of Febal,' saith he.*
> *However, the other saith: 'We do not know such a one,*
> *though the Voyage of Bran is in our ancient stories.'*

> *Then Nechtan leaps from them out of the coracle. As*
> *soon as he touched the earth of Ireland, forthwith he*
> *was a heap of ashes, as though he had been in the earth*
> *for many hundred years.*

Bran now realises that they have been gone for longer than he could possibly have imagined. From the coracle floating offshore, he tells of his adventures, even taking the trouble to inscribe these also in ogham script on stones, throwing the inscribed tablets to shore. Then he sails off sadly with his remaining men.

> *And from that hour his wanderings are not known.*

Mael Dúin

The Voyage of Mael Dúin has some splendid examples of fearsome experiences, which must have made listeners shudder. Mael Dúin sets off initially on a journey of revenge against those who slew his father, but his boat gets blown wildly off course. He and his crew journey from one strange island to the next, finding ever more threatening sights at each landing. Take for example, The Island of the Monstrous Ants:

> *As soon as it was light they saw land and made*
> *towards it. While they were casting lots to know who*
> *should go and explore the country, they saw great*
> *flocks of ants coming down to the beach, each of them*
> *as large as a foal. The crew judged by their numbers,*

and by their eager and hungry look, that they were
bent on eating both ship and crew; so they turned
their vessel round and sailed quickly away.

  Their multitudes countless, prodigious their size;
  Were never such ants seen or heard of before.
  They struggled and tumbled and plunged for the prize,
  And fiercely the famine-fire blazed from their eyes,
  As they ground with their teeth the red sand of
    the shore!

(Trans: PW Joycwe, in *Old Celtic Romances*, 1920)

A water monitor on Trinidad –
was this the creature seen by *Mael Dúin*?

Ants as large as foals? They sound very like the water monitors that are found on the islands of Trinidad and Tobago. Did a sailor who had actually seen these bring that description to Ireland? If so, it would certainly have been noted by the storytellers as good material.

Another creature encountered by Mael Dúin and his men is even more daunting:

> *A horrible monster, with blazing eyes,*
> *In shape like a horse and tremendous in size,*
> *Awaiting the curragh, they saw;*
> *With big bony jaws*
> *And murderous claws,*
> *That filled them with terror and awe:*
> *How gleeful he dances,*
> *And bellows and prances,*
> *As near to the island they draw;*
> *Expecting a feast—*
> *The bloodthirsty beast—*
> *With his teeth like edge of a saw:*
> *Then he ran to the shore,*
> *With a deafening roar,*
> *Intending to swallow them raw:*
> *But the crew, with a shout,*
> *Put their vessel about,*
> *And escaped from his ravenous maw!*

Allowing for poetic licence, this sounds very like a Komodo dragon, found on the Indonesian islands. These fearsome creatures can reach up to ten feet in length and weigh over 300 pounds, and would have terrified anyone seeing them for the first time.

The islands of Trinidad and Tobago, not to mention Indonesia, are certainly far distant from our shores, but another land, somewhat closer, is a little easier to identify. From a distance, Mael Dúin hears roaring and thundering like that of a giant's forge, and inhales the smell of fire and sulphur. As his boat approaches shore, danger becomes suddenly evident:

> ... the first smith rushed out of the forge – a huge, burly giant – holding, in the tongs which he grasped in his right hand, a vast mass of iron sparkling and glowing from the furnace; and, running down to the shore with long, heavy strides, he flung the red-hot mass with all his might after the curragh. It fell a little short, and plunged down just near the prow, causing the whole sea to hiss and boil and heave up around the boat. But they plied their oars, so that they quickly got beyond his reach, and sailed out into the open ocean.

This is certainly a gifted storyteller's version of what must have been a frightening experience, as the ship ventures too close to Iceland during one of its frequent eruptions, and they make a narrow escape from molten rocks falling into the sea.

Another encounter is clearly based on a traveller's recollection of seeing icebergs:

> *The next thing they found after this was an immense silver pillar standing in the sea. It had eight sides, each of which was the width of an oar-stroke of the curragh, so that its whole circumference was eight oar-strokes. It rose out of the sea without any land or earth about it, nothing but the boundless ocean; and they could not see its base deep down in the water, neither were they able to see the top on account of its vast height. A silver net hung from the top down to the very water, extending far out at one side of the pillar; and the meshes were so large that the curragh in full sail went through one of them.*

In one of the oddest stories, Mael Dúin and his men find food and drink laid ready for them in a strange building on

an unknown island. A small white cat watches them, while constantly jumping from pillar to pillar, all around the building. The walls are hung with treasure, but when one of his men steals a necklace, the cat leaps at him and burns him to ashes. Mael Dúin hastily restores the necklace and asks the cat's pardon before leaving.

This is one of the few episodes for which an explanation or comparison cannot be found. Why has the food been laid for them, as if they were expected? What does the white cat symbolise, and why is it essential to record that it spends its time leaping from pillar to pillar? Is it guarding the treasure? Is it a symbol of punishment that surely must follow on yielding to temptation?

On yet another island, they are welcomed by beautiful women who tend lavishly to their every need, while the queen of them all makes Mael Dúin her chosen consort. He, naturally enough, is reluctant to leave, even after they have remained there a long time, but eventually his men persuade him to go. The manner of the story, and the queen's despair at his final departure, have very definite echoes of the tale of Dido and Aeneas from Greek legend.

When Mael Dúin finally returns to Ireland, he finds himself close to the castle of the very men who slew his father. Now wiser, however, after his voyaging, he makes peace and forgives them. Therein probably lies the moral of the tale – travel not only broadens the mind but expands the understanding of human life and the pointlessness of revenge.

Brendan the Voyager

Perhaps the best known of the *imramma* is the voyage of St Brendan, famously recreated by Tim Severin in the 1970s. The original Latin text, *Navigatio Sancti Brendani Abbatis*, is almost certainly based on one of the earlier Irish travel tales, although obviously with many Christian interpolations. Certainly several of Brendan's adventures match with those of Mael Dúin, especially the encounter with the iceberg:

> *One day, on which three Masses had been said, they saw a column in the sea, which seemed not far off, yet they could not reach it for three days. When they drew near it St Brendan looked towards its summit, but could not see it, because of its great height, which seemed to pierce the skies. It was covered over with rare canopy, the material of which they knew not; but it had the colour of silver and was hard as marble, while*

*the column itself was of the clearest crystal. St Brendan
ordered the brethren to take in their oars, and to lower
the sails and mast, and directed some of them to hold
onto the fringes of the canopy, which extended about a
mile from the column, and about the same depth into
the sea. When this had been done, St Brendan said:
'Run in the boat now through an opening, that we may
get a closer view of the wonderful works of God'. And
when they had passed through the opening, and looked
around them, the sea seemed transparent like glass, so
that they could plainly see everything beneath them,
even the base of the column, and the skirts of the canopy
lying on the ground, for the sun shone as brightly
within as without.*

Brendan also comes to the island where food and drink are
placed magically for them in an empty dwelling. In this version, however, the walls are hung with rich harness rather than
jewellery, and a little black demon rather than a white cat is
leaping around, observing them. One of the monks steals an
item, but is discovered. Brendan forgives him, the man dies
in a state of grace, and the little demon is banished. It's an
interestingly Christian retelling of the original. In either case,
though, the circumstances recorded are so strange that it
would make an excellent fantasy film today.

It has become almost accepted belief in the present day that
'St Brendan discovered America', but in reality, this is wishful
thinking. In the first place, the saintly man only thought of

Statue of St Brendan in Bantry, Co. Cork.

the voyage after he was visited by another monk, Barinthus. Barinthus had already been to 'the Land of Promise', which he considered Paradise, so wherever that was located, Brendan wasn't the first to get there. In the second place, this desirable destination is described as spacious and grassy, and abundant in delicious fruits and herbs, which give a wonderful scent to the garments brushed against them. Not quite an accurate description of Labrador or Newfoundland.

It is more likely that Brendan made his way down to Madeira or the Canaries in the south, and on the return voyage was blown by strong winds up to what is known as the northern route. He went by Iceland (the island of smiths) and the Faroes (the island of sheep), and finally back home to tell his story. That is, if it ever happened. It is far more likely to be a Christian attempt to put pagan adventure tales into a firmly religious setting.

Madeira – was this St Brendan's flowery Land of Promise?

STRANGE CREATURES AND STRANGE ISLANDS

Brendan's encounters with a friendly giant whale, Jasconius, are well documented, as are meetings with monsters and strange creatures by other legendary travellers, but we are not told if any of them ever encountered the mysterious seal women. Perhaps not. These tend to stay close to the Irish shoreline and rocky places, enchanting those who hear them with their haunting song.

Selkies

Legends of fierce water horses (*each uisce*), dogs or dragons, either in lakes or offshore, are common enough in Irish folklore. Most large loughs and bays have at least one scaly creature biding its time beneath the surface until an unwary passer-by gets too close. The Shannon estuary, by Scattery Island, is just one example of many. It was terrorised by

Sea creature or half-human?

Cathaigh, a *péist* or sea-serpent, until the monster was tamed by St Senan and banished to Doolough Lake.

Selkies, or seal women, are very different. They are gentle, loving and utterly irresistible if seen in their human form, which only happens when they come out onto the rocks. Then they shed their sealskins temporarily and enjoy the sun, or venture on to the sands to dance under the moonlight. Only at such times can they be seen as truly beautiful young women. Once glimpsed, they are desired forever by the stray fisherman who happens upon their resting place.

Mermaids are more common in other cultures, but occur rarely in Irish legend. There is a carving of one in Clonfert Cathedral in County Galway, but that could owe as much to a skilled mason from overseas as to any local tale. There is a legend concerning a princess named Lí Bán in Ulster, who only escaped drowning in Lough Neagh by being turned into a mermaid, with her pet dog becoming an otter.

> *She also was swept away like the others; but she was not drowned. She lived for a whole year with her lap-dog, in her chamber beneath the lake, and God protected her from the water. At the end of the year she was weary; and when she saw the speckled salmon swimming and playing all round her, she prayed and said—*
>
> *'O my Lord, I wish I were a salmon, that I might swim with the others through the clear green sea!'*
>
> *And at the words she took the shape of a salmon, except her face and breast, which did not change.*

*And her lap-dog was changed to an otter, and
attended her afterwards whithersoever she went,
as long as she lived in the sea.*

There are echoes of Fintan here, Cessair's husband and the
only one of that tribe to survive the flood, but given that the
Lough Neagh region was heavily planted with Scottish and
English settlers, this mermaid tale might be the superimpo-
sition of a different culture. In all other cases, the seal woman
takes precedence in our folk tales and traditions.

What happened when the impressionable young fisherman
fell in love with the beautiful seal woman in her human form,
seized her and brought her back to his home? Well, there are
many tales about just such an occurrence, all with the same
basic theme.

As long as he brought her sealskin back as well, and kept
it carefully hidden from his new bride, she would live with
him and bear him many children. She would never quite lose
her longing for the sea though, and would often be seen on
the shore at night, gazing out over the waves to where her
former home lay.

The tales often tell of children discovering the sealskin tucked
away in an old wooden chest, or a thatcher mending the straw
roof finding it concealed above the rafters. In such cases, the
end is inevitable. The seal-wife would seize her skin joyfully and
flee back to her ocean home, leaving husband and children to
mourn her loss, standing by the sea and calling her name.

It was said that she would sometimes sing to her children
from beneath the waves, calling to them to join her. If they did,

they would live thereafter as seals, by her side. A wise human father would see that they kept close by his side and tried to ignore that haunting song.

A folk tale from County Kerry claims that any family named Lee is descended from a marriage between a seal woman and a fisherman. The same was said of the Conneely clan in Connemara. Roan Inish, an archipelago of small islands off the Donegal coast, translates as Seal Island. A beautifully romantic film of 1994, *The Secret of Roan Inish*, tells the story of a small boy who is swept out to sea in his cradle but, because of his seal ancestry, is cared for by those kind creatures until he is reunited with his family once more. There are many more stories of these graceful grey creatures, reflecting how large a part they have played in our culture since earliest times.

The song of the selkies

Those are legends; but the haunting song of the seal women is entirely true. If you are fortunate, find the right place, and are prepared to wait patiently, you can hear it for yourself. A remote cliff, far from modern life, is essential, with flat rocks below, exposed at low tide, in a bay where the sun shines. Seat yourself on the cliff, a safe distance back from the edge, close your eyes and relax. It may be half an hour, it may be longer, but gradually you will become aware of that crooning, echoing song drifting up from those rocks. Once heard, it is impossible to tear yourself away. When, eventually, the sun has set and the tide has changed, and the song is heard no more, you make your way home an altered person. It's one thing everyone should do at some time in their lives: hear the song of the selkies.

Hy-Brasil

Did St Brendan come across the island of Hy-Brasil? That's the question. Some scholars hold that he did, others are not so sure. Eulogistic descriptions of a sunny, fruitful paradise suggest he landed on that magical shore, but Hy-Brasil is definitely known to be no more than a few miles off the western coast of Ireland, clearly visible from the mainland if you get your timing right. That would be far too close for Brendan or other true travellers to bother with.

Regardless, Hy-Brasil has been part of our myth and legend since earliest times – a mystical island that appears, floating on the horizon, at sunset. Hidden by mist most of the time, some say it appears for just one day in every seven years. Others hold that you just have to be fortunate and believe the evidence of your own eyes.

Hy-Brasil appears floating in mist, often at sunset.

Roderick O'Flaherty, in *A Chorographical Description of West or H-Iar Connaught*, written in 1684, records:

> *There is now living Murrough Ó Laoí, who imagines he was himself personally in O'Brasil for two days, and saw out of it the Iles of Aran, Golamhead, Irrosbeghill, and other places of the west continent [ie Ireland] he was acquainted with …*

What kind of place is this fabled island? It should not be equated with either *Tír na nÓg* (the Land of Youth) or *Moy Mell* (the Land of Honey), both names for that Otherworld where no-one grows old, where there is no anger or unhappiness, and where all is joy. Nor is it like the magical islands that spring up at dawn and then disappear as you try to row out to them. Folklore has it that if you can reach one of these mirages quickly enough and kindle a fire on the shore, it will stay in this world thereafter.

We have only one example of this actually happening: Inishbofin, or the Island of the White Cow, off the Galway coast. It used to appear and disappear tantalisingly, until at last the local fishermen determined to tether it once and for all. Accordingly, when they calculated it was due to emerge from the dawn mists once more, they set out early, and were within range when it did appear. Almost as if it had taken fright at their proximity, the island immediately started to fade from view, but one quick-thinking man seized the pipe from his mouth and threw it onto the sandy beach. That was enough. A glowing fire had landed there, and Inishbofin became part of the Irish coastline for evermore. Think of that when you visit this lovely place, and try to coax the island to tell some of its hidden secrets if you can.

Hy-Brasil, though, is quite separate, a place in its own right. People seem to live on it, certainly, as they have been seen during some of its manifestations. Indeed, those vouchsafed a glimpse over the centuries have described tracks, fields, trees and even cattle. But it can't be visited. It has to be enough just to see it. That its existence was firmly believed in as a genuine landmass is evident from charts and portolans going back as far as the fourteenth century; Hy-Brasil continued to appear on maps right up to the mid-nineteenth century, when it was identified as Brasil Rock.

Unsurprisingly, it has been the inspiration for many novels, and was even chosen as the name for a pop group. And it is still out there, living its own life, tilling its own fields, caring for its own fairy cattle. Maybe they are the little white cows with red horns that sometimes appear in a farmer's field when he has been especially courteous to the Good People? Hy-Brasil isn't telling. It doesn't need to communicate with other worlds. It doesn't mind being seen from time to time by those with eyes worthy enough, but that is as far as it will go.

It is enough to believe in me ...

French map of 1634 showing Hy-Brasil.

An Cailleach Beara and Manannán Mac Lir

One being who can see Hy-Brasil at any time is the Cailleach Beara, who still sits on the cliffs of Kerry, frozen now into stone, but still ever-watching over the oceans for the return of her husband, sea god Manannán Mac Lir.

She is one of the oldest of our mythological beings, and the personification of the third aspect of Ireland's Earth Goddess, the Crone (the other two being the Maiden and the Mother). The tenth-century poem 'Lament of the Hag of Beara' mourns the passing of her youthful days.

> *It is of Corca Dubhne she was, and she had her youth seven times over, and every man that had lived with her died of old age, and her grandsons and great-grandsons were tribes and races …*

(Trans. Lady Gregory *c*.1918)

The Cailleach Beara represents Ireland's unbreakable link with the oceans that surround it.

Even in today's fast-moving world, where technology and science think they have answered all the important questions, she is still honoured, never forgotten. Visit those cliffs where the huge stone sits and you will find fresh offerings laid there to honour her at any time of year. Flowers, scraps of jewellery, coins, buttons, fresh green branches, all lie on and around that great monolith as she silently stares out to sea, immensely powerful in her massive stillness.

Manannán Mac Lir ('son of the sea') owns a magical boat, the *Wave Skimmer*, that can fly over the waves by itself and will take those who know the right words wherever they want to go. The Sons of Turenn in ancient legend are lent this boat when they go to search the wide world for treasures like the Golden Apples of the Hesperides.

So they went into the canoe, and Brian spoke—

'Thou canoe of Mannanan, thou Sweeper of the Waves, we ask thee and we command thee that thou sail with us straightway to Greece!'

And the canoe, obeying as before, glided swiftly and smoothly over the waves …

When Mael Dúin of the *imramma* is voyaging across the ocean, he meets the sea god in his magical boat, and is told of the wonderful world that lies, unseen by human eyes, beneath the waves:

Along the top of a wood has swum
Thy coracle across ridges,
There is a wood of beautiful fruit
Under the prow of thy little skiff.

'A wood with blossom and fruit,
On which is the vine's veritable fragrance,
A wood without decay, without defect,
On which are leaves of golden hue …'

The Cailleach Beara and her spouse, Manannán Mac Lir, perhaps above all else, represent Ireland's unbreakable link to the oceans that surround it. Since time immemorial, the land and the sea have been part of each other, tied together by an unbreakable bond.

Something as strange-looking as a walrus would certainly cause alarm to those at sea in small boats. An unusual visitor spotted at Ardmore, Co. Waterford, in 2021.

Who will come next to our shores – friend or foe?

CHAPTER II

Raiders, Traders, Pirates

T he Fomorians of legend were the stuff of bad dreams, certainly. However, the threat from the North had not gone away with their defeat and banishment. It continued right down into recorded history, and to some extent has influenced Ireland ever since.

THE VIKINGS

The 'people of the fjords' (a literal translation of 'Vikings') had probably been trading with Ireland long before records began, bringing down supplies of the tar and timber that were plentiful there, and taking back in exchange foodstuffs and hides. In later times, when their populations grew and land was scarce, they utilised their matchless seafaring skills to snatch what they needed from more fertile countries: important hostages, who could be ransomed; slaves to work for them at home or to sell on; precious metals, which could be traded elsewhere; and ever-needed foodstuffs.

A very general division could be made between those who went west to Iceland and the Americas, those who travelled east into Russia and down to the Middle East, and those who sailed south to Britain and Ireland, but in all likelihood it wasn't as clearly divided as that, and different tribes from different regions would all have tried their luck here at some point.

A replica Viking ship outside Reginald's Tower in Waterford.

We have heard many blood-curdling tales of these rapacious raiders from the north, and modern television series have done little to alter our general view of their behaviour. Brutal, savage, thirsty for blood and greedy for plundering, pillaging, raping – Ireland must have felt that its last hour had come.

That isn't the whole picture, however. We do need to remember that most of the early accounts of Viking invasions come from the pens of literate survivors: panic-stricken monks whose wealthy monasteries in coastal or river settings were the most obvious target for the raiders. And it cannot be denied that the Vikings did slay monks, or carry them off as slaves. They certainly seized all the exquisite gold, silver and jewelled items that graced the altars. That they also attacked coastal villages – taking hostages, slaves, animals and provisions, and leaving any survivors bereft and bewailing, wondering how they were going to live through the empty months ahead – is also undeniable.

Clearly, a considerable population expansion must have taken place in the Norwegian fjords in the eighth century, causing many younger and landless sons to set off on plunder missions, as this was when raids on the lands further south really started to grow.

The first place to be attacked in Ireland was Lambay Island, off the coast of Dublin, in AD 795. The shores north of Dublin were targeted in 798, and across in the west, there were raids in Connacht in 807. Thereafter, Viking raids were regular, though more infrequent than popular belief maintains.

The *Orkneyinga Saga* gives a very practical view of their timing. The warrior Sveinn Ásleifarson sees to the sowing of crops on his lands in spring, before setting off to plunder in

Lambay Island was the first to be attacked by the Vikings, in AD 795.

the Hebrides and Ireland. Like any good farmer, he comes back to save the hay and reap the grain in midsummer, then returns to raiding until the onset of winter, when presumably he tucks himself up at home and looks over his haul.

To the Vikings, raids were part of life, a sensible way of dealing with shortages of land and supplies at home. And you didn't just gain the plunder, you also increased your standing in society. Being a successful raider gave you status, importance among your peers.

Early raids concentrated on seizing small and easily transportable goods of value, as well as the always-necessary food. Since monasteries here in Ireland were known to hold great wealth, naturally enough they were the first places to be attacked. Coastal settlements, where cattle and pigs could be slaughtered and carried off, were targeted too. Captives were always useful if they could be seized. In swiftly, out quickly, was the guiding rule for the Vikings, and their supremely swift boats and brilliant seamanship made that possible.

Here is something to remember though: they were not the only ones indulging in this kind of behaviour, not by a long chalk. Ireland was at that time a country of many different tribes and kingdoms, most of these at war with one another most of the time, killing, pillaging, taking hostages and making slaves of the losers. Indeed, when the Vikings began to think of settling down here and were making arrangements to live and trade in peace, they were constantly being thwarted by agreements broken almost as soon as they were made, yesterday's friends becoming today's sworn opponents. (It's something that England's monarchs also had to learn to deal with in the centuries that followed.)

The late Dr AT Lucas made a detailed study of the plundering and burning of churches in Ireland, using contemporary sources, and conclusively threw out the idea that the Vikings were always responsible. Of 309 recorded raids between 600 and 1163 AD, he established that the Irish themselves were responsible for half of these attacks. In nineteen instances, the Irish and the Vikings actually joined forces in the raid.

The monastery of Clonmacnoise on the Shannon is a good example of how popular belief can mislead. That settlement is recorded as having suffered no fewer than eighty documented raids over the centuries. Naturally, whatever the date, all of these have tended to be attributed to the fearsome Vikings. That wasn't the case. Norsemen were responsible for only seven of those attacks. Six were perpetrated by the Normans, twenty-seven by the Irish themselves, and no fewer than *forty* by the English. Worth remembering. The monks had chosen a beautiful site to settle, but it was also one of the most strategic points in the country, where the Slighe Mhór, or Great Road, crosses the Shannon, a major waterway. Naturally enough, other people wanted it as well.

Contemporary accounts can mislead or contradict too. One report may say that a monastery or church was completely razed to the ground, everyone slaughtered and the place left a wasteland. Another may record that church silver and gold were taken, and some monks were taken captive, but that the local people came back and tidied things up as soon as possible. It depended on who was recording the event, from what distance of time or space, and whether they were more interested in emphasising the barbarism of the attackers or getting the actual facts right.

Clonmacnoise on the Shannon, a magnet for any raider.

Keep in mind also that capturing people and selling them into slavery was normal practice in most countries at that time. It was common in Ireland, with regular raiding parties heading over to England and Wales (how do you think St Patrick got here in the first place?), as well as warfare between one petty kingdom and another.

The Vikings, however, turned it into big business, having had plenty of practice over a far wider area. They might bring their captives back to their homeland to work for them, or they might take them further afield, perhaps to Russia or the Middle East, to barter for furs, silks and spices. During their reign in Dublin, they created one of the biggest slave markets in Europe. It only came to an end around the twelfth century, when other European countries banned human trafficking. Ireland and Scotland's slave markets were in fact the last in Europe to cease trading.

Findán, slave and saint

The life experiences of St Findán were more exciting than most, since he was snatched as a slave by the Vikings not just once, but twice. A young man of high rank in ninth-century Leinster, he was sent by his father to ransom his sister, who had been taken by the Norsemen. The bargaining somehow went wrong, and he too was taken captive, but released almost immediately when someone on the Viking side pointed out that it was not acceptable to capture someone who had come honourably and openly to ransom another. If nothing else, that does indicate some firmly held standards of behaviour among these wild men of the north, even if they were not quite the same as those of the people who suffered their raids.

But back to Findán. At home once more, this young man was unlucky enough to be snatched again by the Vikings, but this time through the treachery of a neighbouring family that held a grudge against him. Sold on from one Norse trader to another, he eventually escaped when they landed on Orkney to get fresh food supplies. Findán managed to slip away and hide under a tidal rock, enduring the drenching of the waves and barely keeping his head above water, until the boat had left. He then bravely swam to a neighbouring island, joining up with a bishop there, and became a monk in thankfulness. He had clearly got the travel bug by this time, as he later made a pilgrimage to Rome, and finally ended his days at a monastery in Switzerland, where an Irish fellow monk recorded his adventures for posterity.

We are not told what happened to Findán's sister, but we do have the fascinating tale of another Irish princess, similarly abducted. The story of Melkorka, seized and sold into slavery, occurs not in Irish collections but in the Icelandic *Laxdaele Saga*. (It has been utilised in more recent times for several romantic novels, which is understandable, as it is a gripping tale.)

Melkorka, a princess for Iceland

The beautiful daughter of King Muirchertach, Melkorka was captured on a raiding expedition and taken to Norway. There she caught the eye of one Hoskuld, who was smitten by her beauty. Once captured, the practical princess decided that her best defence was pretending to be a mute, unable to speak, and it is as this that Hoskuld bought her and carried her from Norway to his home in Iceland.

Of course, he was married already, and his wife made life fairly difficult for the new concubine; nevertheless, the following year, our Irish royal gave birth to a son, who was named Olaf. Hoskuld's wife now really kicked up a fuss, and Melkorka and the new baby were banished to the care of an obliging farmer, a diplomatic distance from the family home.

Olaf, beautiful as his mother and precociously brilliant, was destined to become a godlike figure, who features in many Icelandic sagas. When he came of age, Melkorka urged him to go and seek out her father and tell him of her fate, even teaching him Irish so that he would be able to communicate easily. Hoskuld (still her owner, even if at a distance) refused to supply his son with the necessary trading goods customary for a voyage, and so the ever-practical Melkorka determinedly married the farmer in whose care she had been placed, since he was willing to provide the required funding.

Olaf did reach Ireland, and succeeded in making contact with King Muirchertach. Speaking to him in fluent Irish, he showed him the gold ring on his arm that was originally given to Melkorka by her father. The king was overjoyed to hear news of his daughter, and pressed Olaf to remain with him, even offering to make him his heir. The young Icelander, however, seeing the king's other sons and foreseeing trouble if he were to accept, declined the honour and set off on his travels again. He asked permission to take Melkorka's old nurse with him, to see her beloved charge once more, but this King Muirchertach would not allow.

In later years, Olaf became renowned not only for his travels and exploits, but also for being the grandson of an Irish king. (It seems a pity that he was not lauded as the son of an Irish princess, but those were male chauvinist times.)

What a story though, and quite probably echoing folk memory of real events. So many young women must have been caught up and carried off across the sea by Norsemen, sold to the highest bidder and thereafter committed to living far from home in a strange and frightening world. One can only hope that some at least found a measure of contentment and acceptance in their new life.

Raiders become traders

As so often happens over time as kingdoms and communities develop, raiding and snatching gradually gave way to trading and intermarrying, absorbing each other's cultures. The bases originally set up by Vikings as overwintering *longphorts* in Dublin, Wexford, Waterford, Cork and Limerick grew into cities. Of these, Dublin, established in the mid-ninth century, was undoubtedly the most powerful, with Viking/Irish kings overseeing enormous trading empires.

These, after all, were the skilled sailors who had penetrated deep into Russia, down to the Middle East and across to the New World. They had amassed immense experience on where to trade, what was most desired there and what would be most profitable to bring back. This they conveyed to their new fellow citizens in Ireland's burgeoning cities, considerably advancing native knowledge and skills.

They certainly would have taught the Irish a great deal about the building of those incredible boats, so light that they could traverse the narrowest and shallowest of creeks, and so adaptable that they could shift direction in just as long as it took the oarsmen to turn on their benches. How many young Irishmen enlisted on board a Viking ship for voyages to faraway lands, returning with their hands full of traded and raided goods, and many an incredible tale to tell by the fireside?

Of course, we had been trading ourselves since earliest times, sending out those goods of which we had plenty – wool, hides, cattle – and bringing back in exchange the items we lacked – salt, wine, iron, tar and timber – from both northern and southern Europe.

The extremely tough stone axes made on Rathlin Island off the Antrim coast were coveted by many in ancient times. We also had our own copper mines down in the southwest, on

The Vikings opened our eyes to a far wider world for trading.

Brow Head and on the Beara peninsula, with its ore much in demand by traders from other countries. Tin from Cornwall, copper from Cork, both soft, together made bronze, that much harder metal desired for everything from swords and pins to decorative work. Many ships must have sailed up to our coastline in bygone centuries, offering spices and wines from the far south and taking away heavy loads of copper ore.

Not done with slavery yet: the sack of Baltimore

Europe in general might have abjured slavery as a profitable form of trading, but other countries had not. The infamous raid on the West Cork coast in 1631, when more than 100 villagers were snatched by Algerian corsairs and carried off to a captive life in North Africa, was vividly commemorated by Thomas Davis in his poem 'The Sack of Baltimore':

Home of the O'Driscolls, sea-lords of West Cork, at Baltimore.

The yell of 'Allah' breaks above the prayer, shriek
and roar;
Oh blessed God! The Algerine is lord of Baltimore!

It was the biggest slaving raid by the corsairs of the Barbary Coast in these waters, and, as far as is known, the only one to have occurred in Ireland. The Algerines normally raided around the Mediterranean, occasionally venturing up as far as the southern English coast to snatch captives from Devon, Cornwall or other easily gained points on the shore. Ireland, though, was not normally on their raiding map. The Algerines knew it well, having friends, and even families, in harbours along the West Cork coast, so naturally they didn't attack.

This shock raid on Baltimore was an appalling, one-off event. The English fleet, based at Skibbereen, should have been on the watch, should have swept down on the invaders and foiled their attempt. But due to disorganisation and lack of resources, it just wasn't ready at the moment it was most needed. Or that was what the officers maintained at the time, anyway.

The men who were taken from Baltimore that night would have ended up as labourers or galley slaves back in North Africa, while the women and children might have become household servants or concubines. White slaves were much sought after in the east, and commanded a high price, so at least there is the chance that they were adequately cared for during the voyage back to North Africa, since it was in the interests of their captors to bring a reasonably healthy group to the slave market. And for some at least, there were opportunities to get on in this strange new world, with a few men rising to public roles of importance, and some women making successful marriages to noblemen.

It was nevertheless a horrifying attack, and very few (only about three) ever managed to get home, when their friends eventually managed to put together the high ransom demanded. Their terror and wretchedness, their sense of loss and despair, is painful to think of.

Yet, at the same period, British, Dutch, Portuguese and other traders were regularly taking black captives from the west coast of Africa and shipping them to Barbados and other sugar plantations, in a highly profitable triangular voyage. Goods went out to Africa, and were exchanged there for slaves. The slaves were brought to the Caribbean or mainland America and exchanged for rum, sugar and spices, which were then carried back to the growing capital cities of Europe. The splendours of London, Bristol, Liverpool, all grew from the profits of slavery, right up to the early nineteenth century. We must hope that the thought of these African captives offends us as much as the thought of white people being snatched by corsairs from the Barbary Coast.

There is some mystery, however, about this legendary raid. Why was this particular settlement picked out? Who led the expedition, and what brought him there? Were the Algerians guided by Irish hands? Were they in fact commissioned to carry out this specific raid? Though it is generally assumed that the victims were unfortunate Irish men and women, the majority were in fact English settlers, placed there with the approval of the English Crown, to lessen the risk of uprisings from the native people on this strategic part of the coast.

Baltimore had been an important druidical centre in early times, and later a seat of the Corcu Loígde tribe, former kings of both Tara and Munster, and so there would always have been a community around its castle, Dún na Séad, the Fort of the Jewels. In later centuries, it came under the control of those seacoast lords of West Cork, the O'Driscolls, who ran it their way, demanding tribute from passing ships and a toll from anyone fishing its waters. In the early 1600s, Fineen O'Driscoll, famed as 'The Rover', was head and fearless leader of the clan.

An old castle towers o'er the billows
That thunder by Cleena's green land
And there dwelt as gallant a rover
As ever grasped hilt in the hand.

Eight stately towers of the waters
Lie anchored in Baltimore Bay
And over their twenty score sailors
O who but that Rover holds sway?

Then hurrah for Fineen the Rover,
Fineen O'Driscoll the free,
As straight as the mast of his galley
And as wild as a wave of the sea.

Fineen was a pragmatist as well as a fierce leader. He could see the way things were going, with the English grip on Ireland tightening by the year. Deciding to back what was likely to be the winning side, he went to London, bent the knee before Queen Elizabeth I (probably gritting his teeth as he did so) and surrendered all his lands. She then knighted him and gave him back his possessions under English rule rather than Irish. This was in fact a fairly common practice among Irish lords who wanted to be sure of holding on to their lands in this new colonised world. However, O'Driscoll's clan was furious at this surrender, and became even more determined to drive the foreigners out.

Being also a notorious area for rebellion, especially during the war with Spain and the battle of Kinsale in 1601, which was a close-run thing, Baltimore was of considerable interest to those English lords doing their best to control this troublesome island. If it were firmly planted with their own loyal settlers, they reasoned, then that would make the task of regulating it much easier – as well as bringing in much-needed income through the fisheries, which the settlers would organise and manage.

And so it was that when Thomas Crooke, an English lawyer, applied to settle a colony there, his request was smiled upon, and he agreed with Sir Fineen to lease Baltimore. Irish inhabitants were swiftly moved out and settlers were brought in, mostly from Devon and Cornwall, with the promise of good land, excellent fishing and a worthwhile way of life. (Exactly the same thing was happening in Ulster, with a deliberate plantation of lowland Scots on what had been the O'Neills' kingdom.)

Soon Baltimore began to prosper, as the shoals of herring and pilchard were exceptionally plentiful at that time. 'Palaces' for gutting and salting the catch were set up, along with the other industries necessary to ship out the produce, such as coopers to make the barrels in which the fish was packed. The town was doing well under the English settlers. Crooke and his people were all committed Calvinists, who hoped that in this Irish setting they would find the freedom to practise their own religion without being harassed by the English authorities. King James, who had succeeded to the English throne on Elizabeth's death in 1603, wasn't particularly fond of Calvinists, but he did recognise the advantages that a strong English settlement would give to that rebellious coastline.

Under the surface, though, trouble was brewing. While the new inhabitants tilled their fields, worked at the huge fishing industry, developed their town and generally went about their daily life, arguments and disagreements were proliferating among the powerful men above. Sir Fineen was still head of the Driscoll clan, but his extended family argued constantly that other relatives had equal rights to his in Baltimore.

Thomas Crooke, on the other hand, felt he had law on his side to hold the town permanently, since he had taken the same precaution as Fineen of surrendering Baltimore to King James and having it regranted back to him. Then there was the grasping Irish landowner Sir Walter Coppinger, who cast envious eyes on this prosperous settlement, wondering how he could get it into his own hands.

Eventually, in 1610, Coppinger managed to persuade the ageing and destitute Fineen to sign an agreement giving him

The ruins of Coppinger's Court where Sir Walter laid his plans to seize Baltimore.

ownership of the town once the twenty-one-year lease was up, in return for a much-needed loan. And all this time, exiled members of the O'Driscoll clan were waiting and watching in Spain, whither they had fled after the Battle of Kinsale. (Fineen's son, Conor, was the last of those to leave, defiantly holding Kilcoe Castle in Roaringwater Bay until the very last minute before fleeing for his life, escaping with his wife and baby son by boat from Ardea in Kerry.)

A complicated and bubbling pot of trouble indeed, and one that would inevitably boil over.

As it did, that night of June 20 1631, when the fleet of Barbary corsairs, led by one Morat Rais, silently anchored in the bay and crept stealthily ashore in small boats to take the sleeping village by surprise. Morat, originally a Dutchman, was a notorious corsair, who had gravitated to the North African shores where he embraced both piracy and Islam. He had a deep and long-standing grudge against England.

Was it in fact a carefully planned, one-off raid for a specific purpose? This theory has been explored before now (by historian WJ Kingston in his *Story of West Carbery,* and by Des Ekin in *The Stolen Village).* Both argue persuasively for this interpretation, and it makes sense. After all, the corsair fleet had even seized a Waterford fisherman, John Hackett, on the way, and used him to find exactly the right place on this complicated coastline of a thousand inlets. They knew where they were to go, and when. Somebody had thought it all out beforehand.

That has to be the explanation. Why, after all, would the corsairs of the Barbary Coast suddenly make an attack on Ireland, something they had never done before? It is reminiscent of that old chestnut of academic discussion: 'Why did the Romans

Kilcoe Castle, held to the last moment by Conor O'Driscoll.

never invade Ireland?' The answer to that, of course, is that they didn't need to. As Tacitus records, they had Irish princes in their entourage when they sailed into Atlantic waters, useful young men who could guide them to likely invasion locations along the English shoreline. Ireland was willing to trade with them, exchange goods and information when required. There was no need to stretch Roman resources further than necessary into a friendly and cooperative country. Exactly the same situation had probably existed with the Barbary corsairs and Ireland – until this sudden and totally unexpected attack.

So who planned the raid on Baltimore, contacting and instructing the corsairs? Was it the O'Driscolls, determined to take back the land they saw as rightfully theirs? (Alas, Sir Fineen had died the year before the attack took place, but there were sons, grandsons and innumerable relatives more than ready to continue the fight.) Was it the exiled branch of the clan, making all the secret arrangements from Spain? Or was it Walter Coppinger, eager to get his hands on the town, and seeing the elimination of the settlers as the answer? In all likelihood, we will never know. It was certainly somebody with inside information, not only on the village, but also on the circumstances of the English fleet at Skibbereen and its inability to respond swiftly and foil the attack.

One fact stands out. The sack of Baltimore took place twenty-one years to the day after the original signing of that lease – which was, you will recall, for precisely twenty-one years. Is that a coincidence? Hardly.

Pirates – or Irish sea lords?

The Barbary corsairs (as indeed the Vikings before them) were both raiders and slavers, seizing goods or people as the occasion offered, and selling both on at the largest possible profit. The terms 'pirates', 'raiders', 'freebooters' and 'privateers' crop up throughout both history and literature, and are often used interchangeably.

Strictly speaking, pirates operated at sea, challenging loaded merchantmen or other likely craft and forcing them to yield their cargoes. Raiders went for swift attacks on coastal settlements or occasionally villages or religious houses up a good river, which assured quick and easy exit to the open sea once more. The term 'freebooters' can be applied to both pirates and raiders, meaning in essence those who operated outside the law.

Privateers on the other hand were poachers-turned-game-keepers, to borrow a simile, lawless men who chose to sail under a country's flag rather than the skull and cross-bones, continuing their pillaging as before, but with letters of marque from their reigning monarch to render them irreproachable. This arrangement was most often entered into when one country was at war with another, and the enemy's ships were regarded as fair game. Of course, privateers were expected to bring back their haul and lay it at the feet of the monarch (keeping back, one imagines, a reasonable share to cover their own costs), who was without exception badly in need of such income to defray the high expenses of war.

There were many examples of notable Irish figures who combined most if not all of these practices, ruling firmly over their own stretches of coastline from their strategically placed castles and promontory forts. They would exact tolls from any shipping that passed through their waters, but also make forays further afield to plunder where they saw opportunity. The O'Driscolls of west Cork, as we have seen, perceived it as their prerogative and God-given right to demand fees from anyone who ventured into their waters, whether passing by with valuable cargoes or coming to fish their rich waters, and perhaps landing briefly to salt their catch. According to an inquisition by the English Crown in 1609, the fee to be paid to the reigning Lord O'Driscoll by any ship simply dropping anchor in Baltimore Harbour was 4d. Fishing rights came at a higher cost:

> ... in money 19s. 2d., a barrel of flour, a barrel of
> salt, a hogshead of beer and a dish of fish three times
> a week from every boat, viz. Wednesday, Friday and
> Saturday and if they dry their fish in any part of the
> country they are to pay thirteen shillings for the rocks
> [i.e. for laying the catch out on the rocks]. That if any
> boat if they do chance to take a Hollybutt [halibut]
> they must give it to the Lord for a ball of butter and if
> they conceal it from him for 24 hours they forfeit forty
> shillings to the Lord ...

Further west, on the Beara Peninsula, the O'Sullivans maintained a strong hold on their stretch of coastline from their fort at Dunboy, taking tolls from those who fished the waters here.

O'Sullivan Beare's castle at Dunboy.

Donal Cam O'Sullivan Beare, the last ruler of his clan, was forced to flee after the defeat of the combined Irish and Spanish forces by the English at the Battle of Kinsale. The 500km march he undertook across Ireland in the depths of winter with the remains of his fighting men has passed into history. Of the 1,000 who set out courageously on that desperate march, just thirty-five reached safety at the O'Rourke castle in West Breifne (modern Leitrim).

In the end, though, Donal Cam, like all the other native lords, had to escape to continental Europe. While waiting in Spain, planning for another opportunity to recover his lands and return to his own country, he was assassinated by an Englishman, while on his way to church. The official reason given for the killing was a personal quarrel, but it was strongly rumoured, and is still held by many today, that the assassin had been sent by the Crown. The Wild Geese had flown from Ireland, and it would be long indeed before they could return.

Queen of the west coast — Granuaile

One there was, though, who never yielded, never gave in, and died peacefully in her bed after a long and triumphant career. On Ireland's western coast, Grace O'Malley, or Granuaile as she is more popularly known, reigned supreme.

This was certainly no ordinary woman. Born in a time when females were regarded as second-class creatures, who simply did not get involved in the world of men, Granuaile broke the mould. She carved out a fighting career in a totally masculine environment, creating an enduring legend that has lasted to the present day. Markedly, she is one of very few women well recorded in those dry English documents of the sixteenth century. Sir Philip Sidney described her as 'a most famous feminine sea-captain', and 'a notorious woman in all the coasts of Ireland'. She was then, and still is now, the archetypal example of a liberated female, exercising to the full her unusual talents as a leader of men, a politician and a sea captain, but also enjoying the pleasures of love, marriage and motherhood.

Born around 1530, from the start Granuaile possessed the instinct to lead and that rare charismatic power to compel total loyalty from her followers. That she was an only child probably contributed in no small measure to her future. Her father, Owen O'Malley, was the leader of his clan and ruler of

The commanding statue of Granuaile at Westport House, Mayo.

the kingdom of Murrisk, a region lying roughly between Clew Bay and Killary Harbour. Her mother, Margaret, was another O'Malley, from the Moher sept of the clan.

Power and leadership were in the genes then, but upbringing played its part too. Her father almost certainly took her on his trading trips and raids along the coast, teaching his young daughter everything she needed to know about sailing, watching the weather and tides. She learned every inlet, every safe harbour. By the time she was a young woman, Granuaile was a seasoned sailor and a confident one too, with probably quite an experience of danger and violence. The fine statue that stands outside Westport House in Mayo shows her with a firm hand on the tiller of her ship.

A local legend records that once she wanted to travel with her father on a trading trip to Spain. Told that she couldn't because her long hair would be a hazard among all those ropes, she cut it all off, dressed as a boy and went on the voyage. That would have been entirely in keeping with her character.

She couldn't quite escape the rigid rules governing women's lives though. The main role of girls of good family at that time (and indeed for many centuries after) was to marry well and thereafter more or less disappear from notice. At the age of sixteen, her marriage was arranged to the wealthy Donal O'Flaherty, whose father was ruler in Iar Connacht (more or less modern Connemara). The O'Flaherty family motto, 'Fortune Favours the Brave', must have resonated almost as sharply with the young bride as did that of her own family, *Terra Marique Potens*, or 'Powerful on Land and Sea'. In any case, she took both maxims to her heart and lived by them all her life.

Swept off to Bunowen Castle in County Galway, Granuaile must have derived some comfort from the fact that she was still within sight and sound of the sea, which had been her companion since birth. Here in her husband's castle, she dutifully produced two boys, Owen and Murrough, and one girl, Maeve, thereby fulfilling at least some of the traditional duties expected of her sex.

Duty and tradition, however, were never her strong points – certainly not where the rules binding women's behaviour were concerned. Since her husband was often away raiding and attacking other clans (his nickname was *An Cogaidh* or The Fighter), Granuaile soon found more interesting things to do than painting, music or embroidery. The harbour at Bunowen was ideal for concealing a fleet of private galleys (in all probability, part of the generous dowry bestowed on the young bride by her father), and soon she was masterminding (mistressminding?) attacks on heavy merchantmen heading to the port of Galway, laden with rich cargoes. There seems to have been no problem with persuading the men of the castle to do her bidding, another sign of her instinctive leadership.

Her boats would strike swiftly, seize their booty and head back to the complex and deeply indented coastline of Connemara, where they could not easily be followed. This, it should be remembered, was before the English Crown had started serious surveys and mapmaking, the better to increase their control over Ireland. Outside big cities like Dublin, very little was known of the coast. Change was on its way, but for now Granuaile lived and worked in an older, simpler world, and could still escape into the unknown.

One of Granuaile's many castles, this one on Achill Island.

Part of her justification for raiding ships on their way to the prosperous and bustling city of Galway was that she, like all Irish traders, was banned from bringing goods there. Only the English or those who had sworn loyalty to the Crown could trade in that port. And so Granuaile felt entirely within her rights in pirating these inward-bound cargo vessels. Since she and her followers were not permitted to sell their fishing catch there (and the waters off Connemara were very rich indeed in fish), they took them down to France and Spain, where there was always a ready market.

Donal O'Flaherty was killed in a battle with the Joyces of Galway in 1565. Granuaile took savage revenge on the Joyces, seizing their castle on Lough Corrib (she never passed up the opportunity to add another castle to her possessions, and held several at any one time). She then returned to her homeland, and many of her husband's followers threw in their lot with hers. Now she operated out of Clare Island in Clew Bay, a place forever associated with the Pirate Queen.

There is another story from this time, relating to a reported shipwreck off Achill Island. Granuaile and her followers, who had been visiting a holy well on Clare Island, dropped everything and sailed rapidly to the location to see what might be found in the way of salvage, but found that the boat had broken up completely and gone to the bottom of the ocean with whatever it contained. However, they discovered a young man, one Hugh de Lacy, son of a Wexford merchant, thrown up on the shore, exhausted and very near death. The pirate queen took him home with her and cared for him, and they reputedly became lovers. Alas, it was not to be for long; he was

Clare Island, long the home of Granuaile, seen from the mainland.

killed by the MacMahons of Blacksod Bay while hunting on Achill. O'Malley immediately attacked the MacMahon castle of Doona, and killed de Lacy's murderers. One of her soubriquets after this savage reprisal was Dark Lady of Doona.

By 1566, she had married again, this time to Iron Richard Bourke, with whom she had another son. It is said that she chose him because of his strategically located fortress of Rockfleet on the Mayo coast, but that may only have been part of the story.

A strong supporting hand in her world of raiding and pirating (she called it 'maintenance') was always useful. Her energetic activities continued along the west coast of Ireland, but English rule was strengthening, and she found herself more and more threatened by a certain Richard Bingham, who had been appointed Governor of Connacht. This was a man who disliked the rebel pirate intensely and did all he could to bring her to justice and the gallows. Imprisoned once for almost two

Did Granuaile marry Richard Burke just to get his strategic castle at Rockfleet?

years, and once being brought within an inch of the hangman's noose, the tenacious Granuaile managed to survive and hold on to her sea kingdom.

However, when Bingham had her sons arrested and thrown into prison to await execution, that was one stroke too many. Grace O'Malley summoned her best galley, packed her finest gowns and sailed for London. Here she more or less besieged Queen Elizabeth I at Greenwich Palace, waiting impatiently

Two powerful woment: Granuaile meets Elizabeth I.

for an audience and talking constantly with the Queen's top advisor, Lord Burghley, until at last she was admitted to the royal presence.

Surprisingly enough, or perhaps not too surprisingly, the two women seem to have got on very well. After all, they were both powerful women in a man's world; both had had to fight for their very survival, and both knew that to weaken even for an instant could spell disaster. They conversed in Latin, as one would not speak English and the other had no knowledge of Irish. Elizabeth was minded to listen to Granuaile's pleas (*release my sons, and get that man Bingham out of my hair and out of Ireland*), eventually granting all of her wishes.

The story of the handkerchief, whether apocryphal or not, is well known: as the Irishwoman, reacting to the doubtless overheated and stuffy atmosphere of the audience chamber, found herself sniffing, she was graciously handed the Queen's handkerchief. Having used it, she rolled it up and threw it into the fire. Shock and disbelief clouded every face in the room, and a gentle explanation came that it was customary to keep and cherish such a priceless gift. Not so, said O'Malley: in our country, we don't observe such dirty habits.

And so she sailed triumphantly back to her beloved west coast, having secured assurances that her sons would be released and that Bingham would be removed. (He came back later, though. He was too good at his job for Elizabeth to replace him.)

Queen Elizabeth I was unmarried and childless by choice, feeling that this was the only way to survive and hold on to power, but Granuaile somehow found time to produce off-spring in between raids, attacks and other adventures. Her son by Richard Bourke is said to have actually been born below deck on one of her galleys, while her men up above were struggling in combat with Barbary corsairs. Once the child was born, and safely ensconced in his cradle, she is said to have leapt up, donned her fighting garments and stormed onto the deck to turn the tide of the battle. *'Can't I leave you to do one simple thing without me?'* you might imagine her shouting exasperatedly. Her son was always known thereafter as *Tibbot na Loinge* or 'Tibbot of the Ships'.

Another legend of the many surrounding Granuaile concerns the pirate queen returning from a long voyage and stopping off at Howth to take on fresh supplies and water for the final stage of the trip back to Mayo. As the reigning O'Malley, she went to Howth Castle to request the customary right of accommodation and food from Lord St Lawrence, but found that this tradition was not recognised within the English Pale, and the native Irish were definitely not welcome.

Barred from the gates, she considered for a moment, then swiftly kidnapped the lord's grandson who happened to be playing nearby, carrying him off with her to Clew Bay. Of course, this concentrated St Lawrence's mind wonderfully, and he set off in hot pursuit, expecting at the very least to have to pay a hefty ransom. Instead, Granuaile set a *geasa* or obligation on him and on his descendants for evermore, that the gates at Howth Castle should always remain open, and that an additional place should always be set at the dining table for an unexpected guest. This he agreed to, and the custom is still observed to this day. A true story then, rather than a legend.

Granuaile is said to be buried on Clare Island.

We don't know exactly when Granuaile, queen of the western seas for so many years, left this life, but it was probably around the same time as Queen Elizabeth I, in 1603. The place of her death is likely to have been Rockfleet Castle (where, famously, it is said that the hawser of her favourite galley was fed through a doorway high up on the walls, and tied to the foot of her bed, so that if anyone interfered with it, she would be the first to know). She is probably buried in the O'Malley tomb at the abbey on Clare Island, though this has never been certain. Wherever or not this was her resting place, her formidable will would have made sure it was within sight of the western sea, her spiritual and physical home throughout her life.

Sea-pirate, she-pirate, warrior queen, leader of men, devoted mother to her land and to her children, Grace O'Malley or Granuaile lives on in song and story, legend and folklore. Myriad boats are named after her (including the Irish Lights service vessel), and there is even a Grace O'Malley gin to be found in off licences, doubtless intended to be stored in many a yacht's locker. To use that classic Irish phrase: *Ní bhéidh a leithéid arís ann* – we shall not see her like again.

Roaringwater Bay, with Leamcon Castle in the background.

CHAPTER III

Making a Living From the Sea

I n earlier times, to make a living, or indeed to survive at all, in a coastal community here meant making the most of every single opportunity and source. Whether it was fishing or collecting cockles, gathering seaweed or searching for useful things tossed up on the shore, every little thing counted.

On our offshore islands, this was even more the case, since they could depend only on the sea, not having a hinterland on which to call when times became desperate. Children learned the all-important skills of casting a line or a net as soon as they could walk, while elderly men and women collected scraps of wood thrown on the shore by the waves, to use in making a warm fire. Many a home or the furniture in it was built from larger pieces of timber washed up by the sea. Nothing was ignored, nothing was wasted. The commonest Irish surname, Murphy, is said to stem from *Mur-chú* or 'Hound of the Sea', indicating someone whose skill and knowledge on the open water was notable.

FISHING

Fishing from the shore, from rocks and promontories, was a way of life, and saved many a community from starvation in famine times. Shellfish and molluscs were also eagerly sought. Indeed, these natural resources saved many a coastal community from starvation during the Great Famine – so much so that there was an antipathy to touching such food afterwards, because of the memories it held. It took until the late twentieth century for seafood to become a top item on a fashionable menu, rather than being dismissed as 'famine food'.

Going further out required the possession of a boat, and those who could make their own currachs would have no problem in finding an eager team to help them cast nets and haul catch in. The herring industry kept generations busy, but before that it was pilchards, which were so plentiful around our coast in the sixteenth and seventeenth centuries that men of means set up fish 'palaces' (the origin of the word is unclear, but may come from the term used in Devon and Cornwall for cellars where fish was stored) in key locations. Local people would be employed to gut, salt and pack these in barrels for shipment to France, Portugal and Spain, where they were much in demand for Catholic fast days. It was probably Ireland's most profitable export at that time, and provided plentiful local employment, both in the catching and the subsequent processing.

Associated industries like cooperage – making barrels to hold the salted fish – and making and mending nets should not be forgotten either, nor indeed the sourcing of the materials to make these. Salt had always been a valuable and vital product, brought in from the coasts of France and Spain, and they must have used plenty of it in the pilchard industry.

The actual catching of the fish required a 'huer' or caller, situated on a high vantage point above the sea, where the shoals could be seen more clearly. There were cases of local farmers objecting to the 'huer' trespassing on their land, and trying to drive them off, but this was strongly discouraged by the landlords who did not want to have their income damaged by a loss in pilchard catches.

In the seventeenth century, Sir William Hull, an English settler who lived at Leamcon Castle on Roaringwater Bay in West Cork, built a pilchard palace near Crookhaven. Here the fish was salted or smoked, and then barrelled for export. Despite the fact that his industry gave work to many people in the surrounding area, Sir William was not popular in the region. During the Rebellion of 1641, the locals rose against him as one, attacking his household, burning his property to the ground and carrying off all his goods. The aggrieved lord naturally made his woes known to the English Crown without delay:

Fishing was a way of life here.

Sir William Hull, knight, a Bryttshe protestant, duly sworn and examined before us, deposeth and sayeth that on or about the fifthe days of December laste past and divers tymes since the beginnings of this rebellion in Ireland he loste, was robbed and forciblye dispoyled of his goods and Chattells to the severall values following viz value of £7679 besides the proffitts of his lande and leases worth £1148 per ann …

Some graphic details of the stirring events follow:

Besides after the Rebells were beaten out of the towne and a ship Imployed then to bring away the distressed people (being almost famished), the Captaine of the ship, Captn. Cole by command (as he pretended from the parliament), fired and burnt bothe Castell and

Towne of Crookhaven with all the fishing sellers which cost above £3,500 the buyldinge and so left the Towne of Crookhaven and lands to the rebels dispose, from thence this ship went to Lymcon to reliev and carry-awaye Sir William Hull's eldest sonn and family and the rest that wer in the same distress that Crookhaven was, by being kept in by all those saide Rebells and many more assembled, the aforesaid Captaine firing and burninge Lymcon Castell and also the towne of Scull belonging to the saide Sir William Hull knight and so left those lands and the other lands following in the possessions of the rebels as they withheld it before from the beginning of the rebellion.

There were pilchard palaces all around the southwest coast, from Waterford to Kerry, and occasionally on other parts of the coast, where shoals would turn up for a year or two before moving on. However, by the mid-eighteenth century, the fish were not coming in the same numbers anywhere, and the industry gradually fell into decline. You can still find ruins of old palaces though, if you know where to look. They are found near the shoreline, where the catch would have been landed, old stone buildings on flat ground.

The most distinctive feature that may remain is the 'pressing wall', with a horizontal line of square holes that held beams. The other ends of these beams were weighted, to press down on the fish to extract the oil. This was very valuable, with a multitude of uses, from lighting lamps to treating leather.

The surviving wall of a former pilchard 'palace' at Baltimore.

Other fishermen made their living from catching lobsters to sell in harbour markets. The inhabitants of the southwest coast of Cork, around Roaringwater Bay, specialised in this type of fishing, using specially designed boats in which they could live for weeks on end. This catch would always sell well in the garrison towns around the southwest coast, where officers and ladies enjoyed such luxuries. It was hard work though, often involving staying away from home for long periods, in all kinds of weather.

One opportunity for adventurous young men living within reach of a port was to join English fleets sailing to the Grand Banks of Newfoundland for the fishing season.

> *In eighteen hundred and forty-six,*
> *On March the eighteenth day,*
> *We hoisted the flag to the top of the mast,*
> *And for Greenland bore our way, brave boys,*
> *And for Greenland bore our way!*

> (Traditional song)

Lobster pots tell the story of an old coastal industry.

Fishermen from the Basque region knew of these rich fishing waters from as far back as the fifteenth century, when it was called Bacalao, 'the land of the codfish'. In Irish, tellingly, Newfoundland is known as *Talamh an Iasc*, or 'the Land of the Fish'. Boats from Italy, Spain, Portugal and France were first to make the testing voyage into this inhospitable region, but English ships soon followed. Waterford, a busy international port, was a favoured last stopping point for these fishing fleets, an opportunity not only to stock up on long-lasting food supplies such as salted beef and pork, but also to recruit local help to work with them for the season in the far north.

Research has shown that the majority of these raw recruits came not only from the environs of Waterford, but also from upriver, from along either the Barrow, the Nore or the Suir, the three sister rivers that meet at the harbour. Many a farmer's son, seeing little opportunity for a living on the meagre family

FOR ST. JOHN'S NEWFOUNDLAND,
TO sail from WATERFORD on or about the 25th JULY,
The well known fast sailing BRIG,

"RATCHFORD."

3

CAPTAIN FLAVIN.

For Freight or Passage, apply to
JAMES KENT.

Waterford, June 1844.

holding, would have signed up at a small recruiting agent's office in a place like Graiguenamanagh, Kilkenny, Clonmel or Carrick-on-Suir. Packing his bundle and saying his goodbyes to those staying behind, he would tramp his way down to the quays of Waterford.

Many such young men might not ever even have seen the sea before, much less had any experience of dealing with vast catches of fish in an icy climate. But they learned, probably brutally, on the job.

> In the stormy seas, and the living gale,
> Ay, and in the gear that I was wearing,
> Sailed ten thousand miles, caught ten million fishes,
> As we hunted for the shoals of herring ...

(Traditional song)

Some would live on shore in Newfoundland or Nova Scotia, gutting and salting, while others sailed the grey, freezing waters, handling the nets. A few might join the sealing boats that went even further north, to the regions of almost permanent ice, or the whaling ships, which were always in need of crew. They went for the summer and came back in the winter, or stayed over the winter in the north and came back a year or two later. Newspapers of the time are full of reports on the return of boats from the fisheries with huge stocks of salted fish for sale.

Sometimes the news was bad though, telling of boats on sealing trips that had become crushed in the ice, leading to tragic loss of life.

EDWARD DOWNES
Queen Street, Waterford,
HAS this day received *ex Reliance*, Captain Do-
NANE, direct from Newfoundland
3,262 Quintals of Newfoundland Cod Fish
500 ditto   Labrador.
which he will dispose of to the Trade on reasonabl
terms.
Waterford, November 18, 1845.

Disaster could strike closer to home too, just when those on board were relaxing and beginning to think of landing. One brig returning to Waterford from Newfoundland in 1799 was seized by French privateers off Dungarvan and taken into Brest. One hopes the crew got home eventually.

Rudyard Kipling's 1897 novel *Captains Courageous* vividly evokes the life on board a fishing schooner off Newfoundland, as experienced through the eyes of Harvey Cheyne, a spoiled rich boy. Swept overboard from a liner by a freak wave, he is rescued by a fishing boat, the *We're Here* out of Glouces-ter, Massachusetts, and is forced to work his passage for the season with the rest of the crew. Gradually he learns the craft, and appreciates for the first time just how demanding and exhausting this life can be. Several Irish fishermen appear in the tale, including Long Jack from Galway, who literally teaches him the ropes:

> *Things at the sea that ivry man must know, blind, drunk or asleep! 'Tis dollars and cents I'm putting in yer pocket, ye skinny little supercargo, so that fwhin ye've filled out a little, ye can ship from Boston to Cuba, and tell thim Long Jack larned ye.*

There is so much vivid detail that surely Kipling himself must have been on such a voyage: the fogs that descend, forcing them to ring the boat's bell constantly to avoid being run down by larger ships; the instinctive knowledge of Captain Disko of where the fish are likely to be, because by now he can think like a cod; the exhausted crew working round the clock to clean, salt and pack the catch; the seascape of the legendary Grand Banks themselves:

> ... *a triangle two hundred and fifty miles on each side – a waste of wallowing sea, cloaked with dank fog, vexed with gales, harried with drifting ice, scored with the tracks of the restless liners, and dotted with the sails of the fishing fleet ...*

When the *We're Here* finally and triumphantly packs the very last salted fish that can be fitted into the hold and turns for home, the first of all the fleet to do so, she weaves a ceremonial passage among the rest of the boats:

> *At last she cleared decks, hoisted her flag,—as is the right of the first boat off the Banks,—up-anchored, and began to move. Disko pretended that he wished to accomodate folk who had not sent in their mail, and so worked her gracefully in and out among the schooners. In reality, that was his little triumphant procession, and for the fifth year running it showed what kind of mariner he was. Dan's accordion and Tom Platt's fiddle supplied the music of the magic verse you must not sing till all the salt is wet:*

> *'Hih! Yih! Yoho! Send your letters raound!*
> *All our salt is wetted, an' the anchor's off the graound!*
> *Bend, oh, bend your mains'l, we're back to Yankeeland—*

With fifteen hunder' quintal,
An' fifteen hunder' quintal,
'Teen hunder' toppin' quintal,
'Twix' old 'Queereau an' Grand.'

The last letters pitched on deck wrapped round pieces of
coal, and the Gloucester men shouted messages to their
wives and womenfolks and owners, while the We're
Here *finished the musical ride through the Fleet, her*
headsails quivering like a man's hand when he raises it
to say good-by.

When at last they reach Gloucester, and Harvey can let his grieving parents know that he is in fact still alive, he is not the same boy who went overboard from that liner. He has grown up the hard way. It must have been much the same for those country lads from Ireland who joined fishing boats heading north to those icy fishing grounds. Whether they came home or stayed on, they would never be the same again.

Seaweed

The coastal dwellers of Ireland have always known the value of seaweed, whether as a foodstuff or as a potent fertiliser for poor land. It has been harvested for hundreds and probably thousands of years, and still today is gathered to enrich gardens and fields. On the Aran Islands, where good, deep earth is scarce, the 'lazy beds' for growing crops can still be seen,

Seaweed has been collected all round our coast for many generations.

with their base layer of seaweed over the thin turf, and the precious hoarded soil laid on top. Dulse, or dillisk, is a favoured dish in elegant restaurants, and carrageen moss has many uses in cooking, as well as being a good-luck charm, said to ensure that money will always come to you.

A twelfth-century Irish poem by a monkish scribe encapsulates in almost-haiku style the simple life lived on the shore:

> *Seal ag buain duilisg so charraig*
> *seal ag aclaidh,*
> *seal ag tabhairt bhídh do bhoctaibh,*
> *seal i gcaracair.*

> *A while gathering dulse from the rock*
> *a while fishing,*
> *a while giving food to the poor,*
> *a while in a cell.*

Where there was no suitably rocky shore, special seaweed 'farms' were created, as far back as medieval times. These were made by placing beds of flat stones on the tidal reaches of the shore to encourage the growth of the plant, with narrow paths left between the beds to aid in harvesting.

The value of seaweed to industry were increasingly recognised as time went on, and a market grew beyond immediate everyday needs. Kelp, for example, when burnt in special kilns, provided the special ashes used for glassmaking, pottery glazing and the manufacture of soap. Merchants in a town would buy the loads carried up from the shore or rowed over from the islands by hardworking hands, and sell it on to factory managers.

> *Galway, October 23, 1766. Yesterday in the afternoon arrived here from Arran a large boat with several Passengers on board. In their Passage they met with so violent a storm that they were obliged to throw five Live Sheep and near five Tons of Kelp overboard.*

Under the ancient Brehon laws, there was normally a common right to any seaweed cast up on the shore. The ownership of organised 'productive rocks' (i.e. rocks placed in the right location to encourage edible seaweeds to grow) usually remained with the person who placed those rocks. Such a food source

SEA-WEED FOR SALE.

TO BE SOLD, for One Year, the Seaweed and Sea-wreck of the Shore of the Lands of Attythomas-revagh, at SALT HILL, near Blackrock Galway.

Any one wishing to buy it will get all particulars by applying to Mr. Pat Morris, Upper Dominick-st., Galway.   14th September, 1852 could add an impressive three cows to the value of a coast-line holding. That is quite a jump in appraisal, illustrating the importance of the crop.

In later centuries, when seaweed was much in demand by industry, individual families jealously protected their 'harvesting rights' on a particular strand or shoreline. One such case concerned a Mrs Hamilton at Balbriggan in 1876, who applied for a lease of the foreshore that abutted her land:

> *Upon this application becoming known, it created*
> *great excitement and consternation, and memorials,*
> *signed by between 500 and 600 of the inhabitants of*
> *the district of all classes and denominations were at*
> *once forwarded to the Board of Trade, praying that no*
> *lease which would exclude the public from the use of the*
> *shore would be granted.*

The *Drogheda Argus* congratulated the opposers

> *... on having defeated this outrageous attempt, backed*
> *as it was by powerful political influence, to exclude the*
> *public from the use of the seashore, which would have*
> *deprived hundreds of poor people of their means of*
> *livelihood in gathering seaweed for sale.*

The women of Kerry went even further afield in turning sea-weed into income. It was recorded by Mrs Morgan O'Connell in 1892 that she remembered ladies borrowing each other's voluminous and elegant hooded cloaks for trips over to Spain to sell their harvest of laver in the markets there. This seaweed – purplish-pink, silky and almost transparent – was very popular there, as indeed it still is here in Ireland, where delicious laver bread is available in good food stores.

Doesn't the story throw up wonderful images? Those Kerry girls stepping on board one of the trading or fishing boats at Tralee or Dingle and heading down across the Bay of Biscay to northern Spain? There they would give the local customers in the marketplace some cheerful backchat, before finding another boat heading north and back home. They evidently didn't trust the sailors to do their trading for them and bring back the doubloons safely.

What has the sea thrown up?
Flotsam, jetsam and wreckage

Naturally enough, jetsam thrown up on the shore, perhaps swept from the deck of a ship during a storm, has always been a plus to shore dwellers. More than that, it was often desperately needed. The wreckage from a lost vessel – timbers, spars, iron, copper – was also welcome bounty. Many a simple hut or cottage was built with planks from a wrecked ship, and smaller scraps of wood became furniture or fed the household fire.

After a storm, everyone looked out for barrels and boxes that might contain foodstuffs. Such finds could mean plenty rather than scarcity on the family table, for a while at least. Flotsam (i.e. that found floating on the sea rather than swept to shore) could be retrieved by skilful hands in local boats.

There was a wonderful haul on the Blasket Islands at the beginning of the First World War, when a huge load of fine timber planks, clearly a cargo from Canada heading for an English port, was washed into the bay. Every man who could handle an oar was out there all day, bringing it ashore in triumph. Around the world, times were bleak, and the circumstances that created flotsam were usually tragic, but on the Blaskets the benefits they brought were undeniable:

> *The war changed people greatly. Idle loiterers who used to sleep it out till milking-time were now abroad with the chirp of the sparrow gathering and ever gathering. There was good living in the Island now. Money was piled up. There was no spending. Nothing was bought. There was no need. It was to be had on the top of the water – flour, meat, lard, petrol, wax, margarine, wine in plenty, even shoes, stockings and clothes. Not a house in the Island but a store-room was built beside it to keep the gatherings, and without any exaggeration when you entered one of them you would think you were in a big town, with all the barrels of flour piled on top of one another, tins of petrol and every sort of riches; and when the old man or the old woman came round, all they had to do was make for the barrels of wine and help themselves to a draught. Buyers were coming from all parts of Kerry to buy the wood, to buy the wax and every sort of oil, so that money was being made rapidly.*

(Maurice O'Sullivan, *Twenty Years A-Growing*)

It wasn't always as easy as the Blasket Islanders found it, however. If a ship was wrecked or driven onto rocks close to the shore, the coastguard would be alerted and efforts would be made to save the cargo for the owners. That was unless the local people got there first. Always living close to the edge of survival, these coastal dwellers were not likely to listen to the harangues of well-fed Crown officials.

The wreck of the schooner *City of Limerick* in 1833 is a good example. Heading out to sea one winter night, she was hit by a storm and swept on to Ballybunion strand.

For some minutes before this the prominent points of the coast were covered with hundreds of the peasantry, anxiously watching the fate of the vessel, and so soon as she struck they rushed down upon the sand, where the ill-fated schooner was already dashing to pieces at each succeeding shock from the combined force of both elements. The master, mate, and crew escaped to shore with no other casualty but the fracture of a limb to one of the latter, but as soon as those shipwrecked mariners gained terra firma, the peasantry surrounded them, knocked down the master, robbed him of a small parcel he had saved from the wreck, deprived the mate of his watch, and attempted also to strip the unfortunate sailors …

As the bottom of the vessel had broken up, several puncheons of the whiskey floated towards shore, and those were eagerly broached by the crowds assembled, when the coastguards, striving to cover the property

from absolute ruin and spoliation, fired on the
plunderers, by which one man was shot. This inflamed
the passion of the wreckers to desperation, and they
made a simultaneous attack on the small coast guard
party who were obliged to fly for their lives.

Then commenced a scene of indiscriminate wreck
and plunder – axes, sledges and saws were employed to
cut up the schooner's decks and get at the residue of the
cargo, consisting of beef, pork, bacon and butter, which
they hurried away into the interior on horses, cars, etc,
with perfect impunity.

(*Freeman's Journal*, 6 December 1833)

In the years of the Great Famine, those living on the coast became, understandably, even more desperate. When the *Susquehanna*, en route from America to Liverpool, was driven ashore near Ballycotton, County Cork, in 1846, local residents had been on the watch from the moment she was first sighted. They immediately started stripping her, taking all the copper from the boat's bottom, and boring holes into her sides to get at the cargo.

In 1859, the ship in which William Jenkin was travelling to Cork ran aground by the Old Head of Kinsale.

When the water ebbed, the vessel was left almost dry.
By this time, a great number of robbers had assembled
on the shore, and attempted to board the vessel. Having
observed that the captain had secured some silver
spoons in his pocket, they endeavoured to cut off the
skirt of his coat in order to obtain the property, but

were prevented. But when we got into our quarters, they plundered us of every article that we had carried on shore with us. I was apprehensive that the robbers would have murdered us, but providentially a party of soldiers came to our assistance; they fired upon the plunderers and killed four of them, which intimidated the rest, and they dispersed.

From the point of view of authority, such illegal behaviour could not be condoned; on the other hand, it is as well to remember just how hard the lives of these local coast dwellers were. They had little choice but to take advantage of the slightest opportunity to improve their living conditions, whether by commandeering foodstuffs or by seizing goods to sell on.

There is a most entertaining story from Wexford, where the brig *Zeno* was wrecked in December of 1843. The coast guards and the soldiers of the local unit managed to save the cargo, which included bales of linen, calicoes, and sails, and put it in store under guard. Despite these precautions, while the guard was watching the safety of the sails, which had been laid out in front of the store to dry, a window at the back was broken, and seven or eight cartloads of goods skilfully extracted. By the time the alarm was given, it was too late to pursue the offenders. Some days later, one of the coast guards was driving a pony and trap along the road and saw lengths of cotton spread on a hedge to dry. He immediately went into the field, but just as speedily two men appeared and, dividing the cloth between them, ran in two different directions. You couldn't teach those locals much about evading capture.

The business of a port

On the other side of the coin (or the hedge, you might say), the merchants of any community depended on goods arriving safely, so as to supply their customers' needs. All major harbours and ports, as well as many smaller ones, saw cargoes arriving and departing constantly, whether to fill shelves in a small local store or to be shipped onward to other countries. Hundreds of little coastal vessels would make their way to Limerick, Galway, Dublin, Waterford or Cork, carrying produce from rural communities and returning with those supplies that could not be provided from local resources. *The Prince*, for example, a small coaster that plied between Carrigaholt and Limerick in the 1840s, brought oats, pigs, butter and beans to the city, while the sloop *James Murphy* from Cork carried flour and meal to several different merchants in Caherciveen in the 1860s. At Goleen, near Mizen Head, where supply boats regularly called from Cork, both locals and skippers knew that it was essential to watch the tides, both for tying up at the small quay and for getting away again before the water dropped too low to navigate out into open water.

Merchants in the larger ports also kept good stocks of provisions and equipment on hand, as ships on longer voyages would regularly call in to replenish supplies before heading for distant shores. Many of those goods kept on the shelves – rope, ironwork, oilskins – would themselves have been brought in by cargo vessels from abroad. Butter, salted meats and oatmeal would have come from local providers. The constant to-ing and fro-ing, loading and unloading, kept many in employment in

It was vital to watch the tides when going in and out of Goleen Harbour in West Cork.

multiple occupations: a small child watching the activity on a town's quayside could grow into a messenger boy, a fisherman or a long-distance sailor, and perhaps settle down eventually as a merchant or ship's chandler.

In a port from which ships sailed to the Americas or Australia, there also had to be accommodation, at several levels to reflect all pockets. Cobh (known as Queenstown between 1849 and 1920) had many options for the emigrant arriving, bewildered and not a little nervous, on the brink of a long and frightening voyage. The better-off could stay at one of the town's splendid hotels, where their every whim was gratified, but the majority were grateful to pay considerably less for a bed (or even a space on a wooden floor).

The needs of emigrants – for immediate sustenance as well as for laying in provisions for the voyage – also meant

opportunities for shops and eating houses. Every sailing
from here for the New World created a linked network of
facilities, spiralling invisibly out from the ship itself on to the
waterfront and into the narrow streets and squares behind.

The Queen's Hotel, right opposite the landing stages, was
definitively for the well-to-do in 1850s Queenstown (*Turtle
and other Soups, Dinner and other Refreshments served on the
shortest notice*). Here the proprietor, RP Hams, offered the
kind of accommodation 'to both Families and Gentlemen,
which had hitherto been wanting in the town'. Rooms for
taking coffee, dining, relaxing and even playing billiards were
available, as well as comfortable bedrooms, with the added
luxury of hot, cold, shower, vapour and salt-water baths.

In somewhat less grandiose, but perhaps more affordable
competition, the Italian Hotel on East Beach offered the definite attraction of 'well-aired beds' as well as meals at any time
of day. In the 1860s, a Mr Downes ran a 'Commercial and
Family Boarding House' at 3 Scott's Square, where respect-
ability and quietness were to be had on reasonable terms,
'within two minutes' walk of the landing piers'. He, or his business colleagues, clearly combined the boarding business with
the provision of needful items for the voyage, since another
advertisement announces that emigrants can purchase beds
and bedding 'more suitable and cheaper than in Cork', of R

Swanton, at the same address in Scott's Square. In the 1880s, the O'Brien Emigrant Home provided accommodation for women only, 'but Miss O'Brien can recommend good lodgings to the friends of her emigrants, who will be met at the train by her man'.

The same was to be found in every big harbour around the Irish coast, wherever international shipping called in. Whether emigrating or stopping to refuel, every visitor needed places to stay, places to buy goods. It didn't take long for the residents of these ports to catch on to the opportunities and wrest their own living from the sea.

The pilots

International vessels, bringing loads of timber or fabrics, spices or dyes, food or drink, needed to get safely to their berths inside the harbour, and to meet this need another trade or career for coastal dwellers came into being: the pilot. This man (we haven't so far found any trace of women pilots, but they may well be there somewhere, yet to be discovered) would be familiar with every sandbank, every treacherous rock or reef on the way in from the open sea. He would board the ship well outside and guide it carefully in past all hazards to its final mooring.

On some very long stretches of estuary, two sets of pilots might be on hand: one to take the boat in from the open water, the other to continue its journey up to the harbour itself. At Waterford, for example, where not just one but three rivers come down to meet at the tidal limit, one pilot would take a ship up to Cheekpoint, and another take over from there to bring it to New Ross. It was a 'job for life' for many of these pilots, and one often handed down from generation to generation, sons learning every little trick and danger of the route from their fathers.

A legendary group of pilots were those based on Scattery Island in the Shannon estuary. This little spot of land out in the middle of the bay, midway between Kerry and Clare, has many historic associations. It is linked with a terrifying monster (defeated by a courageous monk but still, it is said, biding its time and hiding under the waves nearby) and also a death-dealing attack by Brian Ború on Vikings using it as a base. In the nineteenth century, it achieved fame once again due to a famous shipwreck, that of the *Windsor Castle*.

The harbour pilots were at that time mainly concentrated at Kilbaha, on the Clare side of the estuary. On March 13

Scattery Island has many tales to tell.

Old houses of Scattery pilots.

1843, their lookout (naturally enough, they always kept an eye on incoming business) saw a strange ship with no masts, about nine miles off Loop Head. The pilots duly went out in their canoes and boarded her, but found not a single person on board. The *Windsor Castle* was on her way home to Liverpool from Bombay, with a cargo of cotton, indigo, sugar and spices.

The pilots managed to tow her safely to anchor at Kilbaha, but there the local people made so many determined efforts to board and plunder her that it was thought safer to move her to the shelter of Scattery Island. After this, a lengthy court case argued the salvage rights to the ship, claimed naturally enough by the pilots who had brought her in. And eventually it was decided in their favour. Each family that had been involved (and it took a lot of them to get the large vessel all the way upriver to Scattery) got a settlement of between £110 and £160. This was used to purchase land on the island so that they could relocate there.

There were also pilots based at Tarbert, on the Kerry side of the Shannon. Constant arguments and accusations flew back and forth across the estuary about one side taking control of a ship that should by rights have gone to the other, and so on. The pilots found time to complain to the Harbour Board about their harsh working conditions as well, as the *Limerick Reporter* noted in January 1886:

> *Mr Brennan an old member of the body read an exhaustive statement which embraced the many grievances which they have to contend with, and also the low rates which they receive for risking their lives in the protection of property ... He said that the language used to them when they came aside some of the small vessels is scandalous. 'They tell us and the Harbour Commissioners to go to h—l.' Mr Harris said that they could not compel a vessel to take a pilot as there was not a system of compulsory Pilotage on the river ...*

There were plenty of complaints about the pilots too, though, as for example from Captain Giles of the steamship *Treneglos*, out of St Ives, in 1883. A pilot named James Cahill was taking it upriver, but managed to wreck it completely on the Bridges Rock. The Board discussed the matter seriously and agreed to suspend Mr Cahill. Then there was the angry captain of the schooner *Agnes* in 1889, who said that when they were about to leave Clare Castle, 'Pat Ahern, pilot, came on the quay and kicked up a terrible row, arguing with the other pilots about terms. The vessel went on a mud bank near the new pier ...'

The captain blamed the incident entirely on the pilots, saying it was disgraceful, 'and a loss to him to have lost a fair wind'.

In the main though, things were fairly well controlled in the Shannon pilot industry, unlike some less-observed ports, where an entirely inexperienced man might try his luck. The *Dublin Daily Express* of 31 July 1876 gave details of an investigation by the Board of Trade into the loss of the *Goldstream*, bound from Boston to Donegal with a cargo of Indian corn, but ending up stranded on a rock at the mouth of the river.

The evidence went to show that the ship left Boston (U.S.) on the sixteenth of June and sighted the Irish shore at Mullaghmore, county Sligo, on the night of the 8th of July. Next morning the signal was out for a pilot, and a fisherman put out from shore, and, as the mate and seamen swore, he represented himself as a pilot, and agreed to bring the vessel to Donegal for £2. He took charge of the vessel, but as she was going up the Donegal river she was sent on a place called the Blind Rock, and became a wreck. The pilot swore he only engaged to take the vessel off a lee shore, and bring her to where a pilot could be got. The judgement of the court was that the vessel was lost owing to the incompetence of William Killery, fisherman of Mullaghmore, who represented himself as a pilot for the Donegal river, and in whose charge the vessel was when she got on shore. The court, furthermore, held the master free of blame, and returned him his certificate. The court also called attention to the want of a properly licensed pilot in Donegal Bay.

A Cork pilot boat heading out to meet an incoming vessel.

Pilots to guide large shipping into harbours are still to be found everywhere. If you sail into Cork on the Brittany Ferries service, for example, you will see the pilot boat drop off its expert just outside Roches Point lighthouse, so that he can board the huge boat skilfully through a door low down near the water.

He then steers her carefully upriver to her mooring at Ringaskiddy. And if you happen to take the ferry across the Shannon from Tarbert in Kerry to Killimer in Clare, remember to look out for Scattery and remember the pilots who plied their trade here for so long.

So many trades, all connected with earning a living by, from and on the sea. This, of course, marched side by side with another constant demand: that for boats of every size and shape, to carry everything from a netful of herring to gigantic loads of timber or indeed thousands of emigrants. That deserves a separate chapter.

A pilot successfully boarding a large ship down at water level.

A Galway hooker speeding on its way.

CHAPTER IV

Build That Boat Well: Lives Depend On It

TINY CURRACHS TO GREAT SHIPS

Living on a relatively small island as we do, surrounded on all sides by water, boats have always been seen as a natural part of daily life in Ireland, as familiar as the home, the fields or the livestock, and just as essential. To fish for food, visit another community, take produce to a market or head out on a voyage of exploration, going by boat was the only thing to do.

It still is in some regions, where a quick trip on the water takes far less time than traversing miles of twisting roads.

As in every culture, early boats were made locally of whatever materials were available to hand. Ancient dug-out canoes, made from hollowed tree trunks, have been unearthed in peat bogs and at the bottom of rivers, but for the open sea, something lighter and more manoeuvrable was needed.

The currach (or curragh – both spellings are equally in use) is small, light and obliging. It was originally crafted from a framework of flexible branches, covered with stretched animal hides, coated with oil to make them waterproof. Today, with different materials much more easily sourced, a currach is made with laths and tarred canvas, but it is still very much the same in design and ability as it always was, ideal for lightly skimming the tossing waves and slipping in and out of narrow bays between dangerous reefs.

Traditional currachs upturned on the quayside.

At the mouth of Galway Bay, the Aran Islands have used the currach since time out of mind, as have the Blaskets off the Kerry coast. When not in use, these light·craft lie upside down on quaysides, easy to lift off their supports and carry down to the water when needed. The canvas sides could certainly suffer damage on a hidden rock, but even that could be dealt with swiftly by rowers who knew what they were doing, as the writer JM Synge found when staying on the Aran Islands in the 1900s:

> … *bringing round the curragh to take me off a headland near the pier, they struck a sunken rock, and came ashore shipping a quantity of water, They plugged the hole with a piece of sacking torn from a bag of potatoes they were taking over for the priest, and we set off with nothing but a piece of torn canvas between us and the Atlantic. Every few hundred yards one of the rowers had to stop and bail, but the hole did not increase.*

Offshore island communities relied on the currach then, and still do today. They would carry loads of hay or seaweed, even cattle or sheep, from one shore to another. St Brendan used a currach on his travels in the sixth century, and Tim Severin built his own craft to the selfsame venerable specifications over 1,000 years later.

Near the heritage site of Brú na Boinne in County Meath, the skill of making the traditional woven currachs and coracles of that region are still taught by craftsmen.

In Cork, the *Meitheal Mara* community boatyard does the same, passing on the ancient skills to young people.

On a hill outside Bantry, the Kilnaruane pillar stone, dating from around the eighth century, includes one of the earliest known depictions of a boat, thought to be that of Brendan, sailing heavenwards.

That he is aiming for the celestial heights, rather than the sculptor simply having carved the boat vertically for lack of space, is made clear by upright crosses placed below it. One man has his hand on a simple tiller, while four others row sturdily. It is possible that a monastery established by the saint once stood here, but no trace of it remains. The boat does though, carved with such care on the eastern face of the stone. The best time to see it clearly is in the early morning, when the rising sun shines full upon it.

Kilnaruane Pillar Stone, with the earliest known illustration of a boat.

The Vikings, when they settled in Ireland to become traders rather than raiders, immediately set up their own boatyards. When Wood Quay in Dublin was excavated, evidence of just such a boatbuilding yard was discovered. The local Irish people must have watched the skilled Viking boatbuilders at work, and perhaps were drawn in to learn the craft, thus advancing their own knowledge a great deal.

Over the centuries, trading vessels arriving from other countries would also have furnished information and ideas, and by the Middle Ages, Ireland was using several types of boats of various sizes. Irish merchants were shipping out hides, butter and wool, and bringing back iron, wine, salt and more. The imposing carrack, with several towering decks, must have caused a sensation in Irish ports when it first appeared from Italy and Iberia, but we watched and learned. As trade grew, so did our ships.

Where were the materials for these larger vessels to be found? We had the wood for smaller boats, but not the kind needed for major projects. Timber, especially the long, straight tree trunks needed for masts, was being sourced from Norway from a very early stage, as was tar, which occurred naturally there. In later centuries, much timber came from Canada. Iron to make nails, rivets, anchors and so on came from Britain. Sails, though, were made locally.

The topic of sails is a fascinating one. Oddly, very few studies of boat design and boat history bother to mention the sails – how they were sourced, what they were made from. Yet these were the essential feature of the whole structure, far more important than carved figureheads. Without sails, the ship simply would not move.

Early Viking sails were actually of woven wool, felted for strength. To weave enough fabric to equip just one dragon ship would have taken years. To manage this, the Norsemen and Danes maintained huge flocks of sheep on their hillsides, and it has even been suggested that many of the women carried off in raids on Irish villages were taken back to Norway to spend the rest of their lives spinning and weaving. It was an early example of factory work if you like.

In Ireland, we would have used linen sails at first, since flax has been grown here since time out of knowledge. The skills may well have been brought by those very earliest settlers, who would have seen its use in boats on the Nile. When the Vikings set up their boatyard in Dublin, they might have switched to using linen also, since it was locally available, although wool was plentiful here too.

Sheep provided the wool for sails.

Flax was grown, spun and woven for linen sails.

When *The Sea Stallion From Glendalough*, a reproduction of an original ship built in Dublin by the Vikings, was created recently in Norway, it was decided to use modern sails, as it would just have taken too much time and money to use the traditional wool for weaving the 200 square metres needed. Another reconstruction, this time a copy of the ninth-century Oseberg ship, was undertaken by a group of enthusiasts from both Norway and Denmark, and involved a large group of women spinning and weaving the wool to make a ninety-square-metre sail. It cost around €1.3m in materials and time to create that fabric, but they wanted to see if it could be done. This gives some idea of the time and labour involved in making a ship ready for the ocean in the days before industrialisation. In the mid-eighteenth century, no fewer than nine sailmakers are listed in the directory for Dublin.

When factories made the production of fabric faster and more efficient, sailmakers began to use cotton, shipped in across the Atlantic from the southern states of America. The Malcolmson family, who built a huge factory at Portlaw on the Suir, imported massive quantities of cotton to make sails for their Neptune boatyard in Waterford, a few miles downriver. During the American Civil War, when the price of cotton rocketed, the Malcolmsons switched very efficiently to linen spinning and weaving for the duration, sourcing their supplies from Limerick and Belfast.

In nineteenth-century Cork, the Douglas spinning mills employed hundreds, not only supplying the numerous Irish

Ruins of Portlaw Mill, where the Malcolmson family spun and wove the sails for their own fleet of merchant ships.

In its heyday, Douglas mill supplied all the sailcloth for the British Navy.

shipbuilders, but also shipping their cotton and canvas abroad, to equip boats in England and Europe.

Looking at a picture of a clipper ship in full sail, one can only wonder at the sheer amount of fabric needed to equip that vessel. It has been calculated at around 32,000 square feet, or 9,700 square metres. This could have served well as one of those mathematical problems for nineteenth-century school-children: *If it takes one weaver so many days to make twenty feet of sail canvas, how many weavers and how many days will be needed to get that urgently required new boat off the slipway and into operation?* If the industrial revolution had not come into being, such empresses of the seas might never have been seen.

Everything on the ocean was still powered by sail and oar though, depending on the winds and on human effort. When steam-driven ships began to appear in the nineteenth century, the sail market dropped accordingly, but never died out. Wealthy ex-Navy officers and well-to-do merchants were by this time forming exclusive sailing clubs and having splendid

A clipper ship at full sail.

boats built. They would carry out manoeuvres and exercises, or races for wagers, in the large bays of Cork, Dublin, Galway and more. (The story goes that some of the wealthy with large households would commandeer their fitter menservants to act as crew on their day off.) The demand for good quality sails continues to this day. As does the demand for sleeker, faster and definitely more expensive yachts.

Throughout the nineteenth century, the unstoppable expansion of worldwide trading meant that newer, bigger, faster ships were always in demand, while the localised industries of fishing and coastal trading continued as they had always done. And that of course meant a continual demand for repairs and refits. Large shipyards in Belfast, Cork, Dublin, Limerick and Waterford supplied the needs of the international trade, while smaller ones – often no more than one family, passing on its skills from father to son – were to be found everywhere around our shoreline.

Milk Harbour was for centuries the main trading port on the Sligo coast, and here the McCann family carried on the business of boatbuilding throughout the nineteenth and twentieth centuries.

This harbour lies in the sheltered waters behind Derinish Island, a place we have met already in the first chapter, as the possible home of the terrifying Balor of the Evil Eye. Johnny Rua McCann, who carried goods back and forth between Killybegs and small ports on the Donegal and Sligo coasts,

Milk Harbour in Sligo, where Johnny McCann had his boatyard.

first set up the boatbuilding and repairing business, which his descendants continued until the last of the craftsmen passed away in the early twenty-first century. The McCanns would have dealt with local fishermen and with coastal packet steamers, anyone wanting a new rowing boat or repairs to a venerable one.

Further down on that western coastline, around Galway, a particular type of boat known as a 'hooker' was favoured. They were made in several sizes, depending on the purpose for which they were intended. Today, you can still see examples of the Galway or Connemara hooker, with its distinctive red-brown sail, tacking across the wide expanse of the bay or tying up at the Galway quays.

Mweenish Island off Carna had an active boatyard building these hookers throughout the nineteenth and twentieth centuries. The sails got their colour from the concoction of boiled tree bark that was painted onto them every year to keep the calico weatherproof. Many an anxious wife must have stood on the quaysides after a storm, searching the horizon for a welcome glimpse of that colourful sail.

Indeed it was the sight of just such an Irish boat that inspired a famous song of 1935 by Williams & Kennedy:

> *Red sails in the sunset, way out on the sea,*
> *Oh carry my loved one home safely to me …*

From Heir Island in Roaringwater Bay down to Crookhaven on the Mizen Peninsula in West Cork, generations of boatbuilders made special craft for lobster fishing, called in popular parlance

A Galway hooker.

'towelsail yawls'. These featured a tent of canvas suspended from the mast, in which the crew could cook food and snatch some rest during the lengthy trips they took away from home, sometimes down as far as Dursey Island and up to Ardmore in Waterford. In a good breeze, it also did service as a sail. The Irish for 'tent' is *teabal*, and this became Anglicised into 'towel', hence 'towelsail'.

The long sea journeys taken by these small boats must have been fairly demanding, hauling up and putting down weighty lobster pots, mooring in sheltered bays for the night, running before the wind or sheltering from a storm, seeking fresh water or food supplies. The catch would be sold at markets in Kinsale and Cobh, where there was always a demand for fresh lobster among the cognoscenti of those towns. The crews knew every single inlet, every location of springs or wells (even to the ancient carved steps up to a natural spring in the eastern side of the Old Head of Kinsale), and could sniff out bad weather on the way before there was ever a cloud in the sky.

Travelling around the coast, it is not difficult to spot the remains of old fishing boats, their timbers sun-dried and worn, grass and weeds sprouting up through their sides, with here and there scraps of bright paint hinting at how they looked when they were fresh and new. Every one of these has its own history, stored deep within the traditional shape that still remains even when almost hidden beneath encroaching vegetation.

The bigger vessels required by the growing number of merchants and shipping lines needed bigger boatyards, and we had plenty of those too. Danish Vikings settled on the east coast in what is now Arklow around the eighth century,

Memories of yesteryear: old fishing boats.

bringing their boatbuilding skills with them – skills that have been handed down to the present day. There was probably a small trading port here even earlier than that. Later came the Normans, and by the sixteenth century, there was much trading with the European continent. In the nineteenth century, fishing and boatbuilding were the principal industries in Arklow. The shipyard founded there by John Tyrrell in 1864 is still operated by his great-grandchildren today.

In Belfast, William Ritchie from Ayrshire founded the first boatbuilding yard in 1791, thereby starting an industry that would be identified with the city for two centuries to come. In the 1850s, a new site on the banks of the Lagan River became home to both Harland & Wolff and their main rivals, McIlwaine & Coll. The latter was taken over by Workman & Clark, on the other side of the Lagan, in the 1880s, where refrigerated shipping was pioneered. Harland & Wolff began to create magnificent transoceanic liners for the White Star Line, of which the most famous is of course the *Titanic*. (You can buy T-shirts in Belfast today that state crossly, '*She was alright when she left here ...*')

Having gotten off to a good start with that Viking ship-yard back in the ninth century, Dublin didn't forget the skills learned at the hands of master boatbuilders. Throughout the ensuing centuries, trades related to shipping were very much part of the city's industry. The dockyard on the North Wall was variously known as Vickers (part of the huge Vickers-Arm-strong consortium) or simply the Liffey Yard. In 1864, a Quaker consortium, Walpole, Webb and Bewley (yes, the Bewleys of the legendary Dublin cafes), opened the first large yard specifically for iron sailing ships and paddle steamers, bringing over skilled craftsmen from England and Scotland. The first large iron boat to be launched in Dublin was their *Knight Commander*, which was christened by the Marchioness of Kildare. It was a sailing ship, destined for the Calcutta run operated by Carlyle & Gedes of Liverpool, whose principal, TH Ismay, would go on to found the White Star Line.

Later, the company seems to have split into Bewley Webb, and Ross & Walpole. Walpole's built the famous Guinness barges, which plied Dublin's Grand Canal from the brew-ery to Dublin Port, laden with full barrels for transhipment on to England, and returning with empty ones that had arrived back.

The huge Graving Dock on the North Wall accommodated the Holyhead paddle steamer on its regular run. And there were numerous other shipyards and repair yards all along the Liffey and along the coastline in both directions. Where the

An old canal barge, probably built at Ringsend in Dublin.

Dodder meets the Liffey at Ringsend Bridge, traces of old slipways and docks can still be seen, showing where earlier boatyards once rang to the sound of hammer and saw. McMullan's was in the Ringsend canal basin, while John Clements built lifeboats here for use around Dublin Bay, notably at Clontarf, Sandycove and Sutton, in the first decade of the nineteenth century. Other boatyards around the coast built these too, for the dedicated local teams of volunteers who would head out to help a ship in distress. And it was from a Dodder slipway in Dublin that the enigmatic *Ouzel Galley* was launched in the eighteenth century, sailing off into mystery. We will meet the *Ouzel* again later in this chapter.

One of the major shipbuilders in Limerick was Russell's on the Strand. Russell was a merchant, a ship owner and an industrialist, who owned several mills in the city and utilised his locally built boats for coastal trading. The much-admired *Sea Lark* was built here; unfortunately, it capsized in a severe squall en route from Askeaton to Tralee in 1846, laden with flour, meal, oatmeal and bran. This was during the height of the Famine, and the local people, being half-starved, seized the opportunity to plunder whatever they could from the wreck, despite expostulations from the coast guards and soldiers sent to the scene.

All of these boats in various ports and harbours were needed for expanding trade, and that in turn saw the growth of shipping companies. Belfast, Cork and Dublin all had regular sailings to England and Scotland. The Limerick Steamship Company was founded in 1893 for the Liverpool route. It gradually extended its service to take in Galway and many smaller west coast ports as well, so that goods could be put on board at Ballina or Sligo and get to Liverpool eventually. From there, they could be transhipped on to European ports.

At the beginning of the twentieth century, to cope with increasing demand, the Limerick Steamship Company even opened a trading route direct to Hamburg, and therein lies a story: In September 1914, just before the outbreak of the First World War, one of their ships, the *Sinainn*, set sail as usual on her return voyage from Hamburg for Limerick, with Captain McNamee in charge. She was, however, intercepted by a German patrol boat on the Elbe and ordered back into port. The captain's first instinct was to ignore the command, but he was forced to think again:

> *As a result of refusing to return, the guns of the German ships were turned on his vessel, and he was informed that if he did not act in compliance with instructions, his vessel would be sunk.*

He swung back to Hamburg and was detained in an
internment camp in Germany for the war period.

The entire crew was in fact held, and the *Sinainn* pressed
into undignified service as a coaling ship, only to be lost off
the coast of Latvia in 1916. Whatever cargo she had originally been carrying back to Limerick, it never got there. We
do know, however, that Captain McNamee did finally return
home safely after the war, and resumed working with the
Limerick Steamship Company until his retirement in 1932.

In the mid-nineteenth century, Cork and Waterford were
the undoubted leaders in the shipbuilding industry, producing
one spectacular craft after another at a number of yards.

Cork

Up to the 1850s, Passage West, some way downriver from the city, was the point where
large boats had to moor, because the
river further up was still too shal-
low to accommodate them.
Goods and passengers were
loaded into lighters and taken
up to the city quays, with the
reverse operation bringing out-
ward goods and people down to
Passage West.

On the slipway at Passage West in the
19th century.

145

The growing commercial business of Cork made it a busy place, and several boatyards were based here. The first steamship to be built in Ireland was launched at Passage on 10 June 1815. She was the *City of Cork*, from Andrew Hennessy's yard. Hennessy was harbourmaster in this bustling port, as well as a shipbuilder.

In 1832, Queen Victoria formally opened a very large dockyard here, built by William Brown. Up to eighty ships might be seen anchored in the local harbour at peak times. The *Sirius*, the first steamship to cross the Atlantic, sailed from here in 1838. (She gets the attention she deserves later on.)

The eventual dredging of the Lee channel in the 1850s saw Passage dwindling in importance as a port, while the city's quays became far busier. Today, it rests somewhat on its laurels and its memories, but a maritime museum enshrines the records of its proud past.

Many shipyards grew up in the city itself, utilising the wide banks of the Lee. Lecky & Co built ships for their own business, the St George Steam Packet Co (later the City of

Pike shipyard on the Lee, still recognisable today.

Cork Steam Packet). The Pike family had a large shipyard too, as well as running the City of Cork Steamship Company, which ultimately took over the Lecky business. At its height, Pikes' employed up to 370 men, and the first iron-built ship from a Cork yard was the three-masted *Cormorant* from this company. (We will hear more of the *Cormorant* later.) In all, the Pikes built eight iron ships named after birds: the *Gannet, Pelican, Cormorant, Falcon, Dodo, Osprey, Bittern* and *Ibis*. (One does wonder about the wisdom of calling a boat the *Dodo* ...)

It is revealing to observe the somewhat superior attitude taken by the English papers to this homegrown industry:

LAUNCH OF THE 'PELICAN' IRON SCREW STEAM SHIP

The launch of this beautiful specimen of shipbuilding took place on Tues 11th at five o'clock, at Cork, and affords an instance, in addition to the many signs perceptible every day to a close observer, of the ardent disposition in Ireland to set herself right.

To all those taking an interest in naval affairs, the steady and rapid onward course of this vessel has been a theme of admiration; her after fortune, let us hope, will prove that when Erin's children have those with head, heart, and capital to guide them, they are able to earn a portion of renown such as has been so well won by the British Empire ...

(Illustrated London News, 22 June 1850)

By the 1870s, business was expanding so much that Pikes' divided it into two separate sides: the City of Cork Steam Packet Company, which ran the coastal routes, taking goods to and from different Irish ports; and the Cork Steamship Company, which saw to continental traffic.

Joseph Wheeler had a yard on the Lower Glanmire Road in the 1820s and 30s, but in the 1850s moved to Rushbrooke, further downriver, near to Cobh, where that industry continued up to the late twentieth century. There were many more, smaller boatyards too, especially at outlying harbours and ports like Crosshaven and Kinsale, where there was always business to be had from both fishermen and the yachting set.

Waterford

The Neptune shipyard in Waterford was a vast, family-run business, owned by the Malcolmson family, owners of the enormous cotton mill upriver at Portlaw. They needed their own efficient fleet of vessels to bring in raw materials and send out their woven products, and so set up the shipbuilding and repair operation here in 1843. By the 1860s, they were said to be the largest steam owners in the world.

One reason for their success was the adoption of propellers rather than paddles for steamships, in which they were one of the leaders in the field. The very first Waterford-built steamship was the *SS Neptune*, launched in 1849 at the Malcolmson yard. At 172 feet long and weighing 326 tons, it was at the time the largest ship of its kind in Ireland. We will meet the *Neptune* again later on, since its career, though short, was definitely distinguished.

Another busy yard in Waterford during the nineteenth century was Pope & Co, where the 684-ton *SS Kilkenny* was launched in 1837. It was purchased by the East India Company for the Bombay–Suez run, and was later renamed the *Zenobia*. According to a rather disapproving East India report, she had originally been employed in carrying pigs from Waterford to Bristol. She was, however, one of the earliest steamships to round the Cape of Good Hope en route to Bombay and live to tell the tale, so she deserves some recognition of that achievement at least.

So many ships, so many launches, so many high hopes. Everyone knows the fate of the *Titanic*, but there are some fascinating stories about other notable ships either built in, or built for, the Irish trade, which are not so familiar. Here are just a few of them.

Ouzel, Ouzel, where have you been?

In the autumn of 1695, a merchant galley christened the *Ouzel* (Blackbird) was launched from a slipway on the Dodder River in Dublin's Ringsend, slipping smoothly into the main waterway of the Liffey. Captain Eoghan Massey and his crew were setting sail for Smyrna on a trading mission, with a full cargo of goods. Presumably, the owners (the shipping company of Ferris, Twigg & Cash) and the merchants who had contributed to the cargo turned out to wave farewell and wish her good luck on her voyage. Then they settled down to await her return the following year, hopefully with the results of a profitable trip.

Only … she didn't come back the following year. Nor the year after that. In 1698, three years after the *Ouzel* had sailed down the Liffey, a panel of city merchants met to argue the matter of insurance. After lengthy discussion, it was decided that the ship must have been lost with all hands, since no sightings had been reported since, either of her or of any of her crew. All those who had left on the *Ouzel* were therefore declared dead, and insurance compensation was paid out to the owners and merchants. Grieving wives and families became accustomed to the loss and got on with their lives, since there was no help for it.

Two years after that again – that is, in the autumn of 1700 – what should appear, sailing cheerfully up the Liffey, but the *Ouzel* herself, large as life and twice as natural? The city's merchants rubbed their eyes and stared in disbelief. Was it a mirage? Apparently not. When she had moored and the crew had surged ashore, happy, healthy and entirely unscathed by their five-year absence, a rich cargo of spices, exotic products and rich goods, which looked suspiciously like a pirate's hoard, was revealed in the hold.

Of course, Captain Massey had an excellent story to explain their somewhat lengthy absence from home. They had been captured by Algerian corsairs, he explained, and taken to the Barbary Coast, where they were forced to work for those pirates in their seaborne attacks. Happily, he said, after five years of bondage, a night came when their captors over-indulged in a drunken celebration. Massey and his crew seized the opportunity to break free and take back their ship, still burdened as it was with the takings from the most recent raid. Then, he said simply, what would they do but sail straight home?

Sad to say, not everyone swallowed this clear and innocent account completely. Some even went so far as to suggest that both captain and crew had been engaging in a little piratical business of their own, finding it far more profitable than an ordinary, lawful trading trip. Others murmured that the safe return of every single person on that boat, with no injuries to speak of and with such booty, seemed a little far-fetched.

Whatever the truth of the matter, what was now to happen to this rich cargo? And what of the insurance payments that had already been made to the owners and merchants of the city two years before? The panel that had settled the question of insurance in 1698 was hastily reconvened. In the end, it seems they decided that anything remaining after the ship's owners and insurers had been properly compensated should go into a fund for the alleviation of poverty among Dublin's 'decayed merchants'.

But there was a personal side too! What of the grieving wives and families who had had to accept the loss of their menfolk years earlier? Some had remarried; some had divided the lost one's property among their next of kin. Many a crew member must have walked briskly to his former home only to find the gate shut, and strange children in the garden.

A novel of 1876 by WHG Kingston retold the story as *The Ouzel Galley, or Notes From an Old Sea Dog*. And, demonstrating how the event and the ship became a byword in old Dublin, it even gets a mention in James Joyce's *Finnegans Wake*:

> *carried of cloud from land of locust, in ouzel galley borne ...*

We will never be quite sure what really did happen to the *Ouzel*, but a direct result of its strange disappearance and reappearance was the setting up of the Ouzel Galley Society, a permanent panel to deal with similar shipping disputes that might occur in the future. In the late eighteenth century, this became part of the Dublin Chamber of Commerce. Strange things happen at sea, to be sure, and in a city that is so involved with the sea, it is best to be prepared.

I got there first! The *Sirius*

The *Sirius*, a wooden-hulled sidewheel steamship, was built in Leith in 1837 for Ebenezer Pike's Saint George Steamship Company in Cork, destined for the Cork–London route, which she began the same year. On her second trip to England's capital, she caused no little stir at the quaysides when a fire was discovered on board:

> *Yesterday afternoon at two o'clock, on the arrival of the new and large steam-ship* Sirius *off Alderman's stairs, from Cork, with passengers, goods, and cattle, a fire was discovered in one of the coal bunkers. This had extended so far among the coals that the engineers and stokers were incapable of subduing it by ordinary means, and as soon as the passengers were landed orders were given to tear up the decks. Several holes having been cut with the carpenter's adze, a dense volume of smoke ascended, which caused very great alarm among the crews of the various ships and steamers in the tier. Immediate preparations were made for hauling away, and expresses were sent off to the floating engines of*

The drive shaft of the doughty little *Sirius*, now becalmed at Passage West.

the London Fire Brigade Establishment, between Rotherhithe and Wapping, and at Southwark-bridge. In the meantime the captain, officers, and crew of the Sirius *adopted active measures for the suppression; their own fire-engine on board was set to work, and the hose was carried over several vessels in the tier from the* Express *and* Scotia *steam-ships also belonging to the St George Company, and by the united power of the three engines large quantities of water were discharged into the bunkers of the* Sirius *and with complete effect; for in less than half an hour the fire was got under and all further danger was at an end. The floating engines, with a numerous body of firemen, watermen, and Thames police officers arrived, but their assistance not being required, the engines were turned down to their respective mooring places. On*

inspection, no traces of the fire were to be seen, with
the exception of the recent cutting away of a portion
of the upper deck which it appears can be made good
for less than £5. This is the whole extent of the damage
effected, and nothing whatever ignited below except the
coals in the bunker where the fire was first seen ... At
five o'clock yesterday afternoon it was reported in the
City that the Sirius *had been destroyed by fire, and for*
some time afterwards the subject was the only topic of
conversation. Half an hour before that time the captain
and his officers were at dinner in the cabin and the
crew were engaged in discharging the pigs and cargo as
if nothing uncommon had happened ...

(*Public Ledger & Daily Advertiser*, Tuesday, 10 October 1837)

Clearly, the *Sirius* was a doughty little ship, well capable of handling whatever crisis might come at her; but even she did not expect the challenge that was soon to come her way.

Around the same time that she was being built for the Cork–London run, it so happened that two far bigger steamships were also in course of construction, both intended solely for services between Europe and the New World. It was an unofficial contest, to see who could get there first. The winner would forever be known as the one who established the transatlantic steam route. By chance – aided by a good helping of adventurous David-and-Goliath thinking – the little *Sirius* snatched the prize. Not that she was all that little – at 700 tons, she was more than adequate for the Cork–London run – but compared to the giants being constructed in Britain, she appeared so.

The *British Queen* (British & American Steamship Navigation) dropped out of the running when the company building her engines went bankrupt; but the *Great Western*, designed by Brunel and at the time the biggest steamship in the entire world, was, so to speak, steaming ahead. Her initial voyage was scheduled for April 1838, as the first ship of the new Great Western line.

The British & American company were feeling somewhat annoyed about their *British Queen* losing the opportunity of being first steamship across the Atlantic. Having heard of the good performance of the *Sirius* on its preliminary voyages to London, they had the idea of chartering it, to see if it could beat the *Great Western* and get to New York first. It was a mad notion in many ways, but clearly one that appealed to the directors of the Cork company, since they agreed at once, and speedy arrangements were made.

Brunel's mighty monster was scheduled to sail at the end of March, but due to a fire on board (shades of the *Sirius*) and an injury to Brunel himself, who was on board at the time, its departure was delayed. That gave *Sirius* the chance she needed. A large part of her passenger accommodation having been temporarily removed, to allow for larger stores of coal (and several casks of Beamish & Crawford stout, presumably intended as gifts), the determined little sidewheeler, with the experienced Captain Roberts in charge, slipped her moorings at Passage West at 10am on 4 April 1838, setting out for New York with forty-five passengers.

As the Sirius *passed down the river she was cheered loudly by the thousands of people who lined the shores, and the battery at Rocky Lodge, Monkstown (then the residence of Mr. John Galway), fired a salute. The* Ocean *with Mr. Joseph R. Pim, one of the Directors of the Saint George Co., Mr. James Beale, and Mr. George Laird, on board, proceeded to the harbour's mouth. Then the two steamers saluted by dipping their flags, and the* Sirius *stood her course for the New World majestically, and was watched with keen interest until she finally disappeared on the waste of waters, between two continents, hitherto untracked from shore to shore by any steam vessel.*

James Beale, one of those watching the departure, had a particular reason to be pleased. At a lecture in London back in 1836, he had heard it declared that a steamship crossing to America was as likely as a trip to the moon. Returning to Cork, he rebuffed this theory furiously, and declared that if someone would find a good enough ship, he would supply the coals for the voyage! Which, apparently, he did.

And that coal supply did last out, despite rumours (fake news?) put about in the newspapers that the crew had to burn cabin furniture, and anything else wooden, to make it to New York. In fact, because they had several barrels of resin on board that could also serve as fuel, the *Sirius* arrived with a spare fifteen tons of coal. But the legend persisted, and made useful material for Jules Verne in his classic *Around the World in Eighty Days*, some decades later.

When the *Sirius* arrived, on April 23, after a voyage of eighteen days (a sailing ship normally took around forty), New York went delirious with excitement, and Captain Roberts himself could not hide his delight:

> *We have gained all that we want – at least I have – that is, to be the first to cross the Atlantic, to and fro …*

There was an absolutely wonderful extra scene still to be played, though, incredibly vivid in its descriptive detail.

> *[The Sirius] came to anchor in the North River early in the morning of the 23^d. The news spread like wildfire through the city, and the river became literally dotted all over with boats conveying the curious to and from the stranger. There seemed to be a universal voice in congratulation, and every visage was illuminated with delight …*
>
> *Whilst all this was going on, suddenly there was seen over Governor's Island a dense black cloud of smoke spreading itself upward, and betokening another arrival. On it came with great rapidity, and about three o'clock in the afternoon its cause was made fully manifest to the accumulated multitudes at the battery. It was the steam ship* Great Western, *of about sixteen hundred tons burden, under the command of Lieutenant Hosken, R.N. She had left Bristol on the 7th inst, and on the 23rd was making her triumphant entry into the port of New York.*

> *This immense moving mass was propelled at a rapid rate through the waters of the bay; she passed swiftly and gracefully around the* Sirius, *exchanging salutes with her, and then proceeded to her destined anchorage in the East River.*

(New York correspondent, *Monmouthshire Merlin*, 26 May 1838)

Oh, to have been on deck with Captain Roberts, and see him smile politely and salute courteously as his rival steamed furiously past, knowing it had come second in the race …

The *Great Western* was of course the bigger and faster steamship, and did in fact make far better time. The *Sirius*, however, through the quick thinking and speedy action of the opposition, was the first to make that historic run, and forever after held the title. When she left New York to return to Cork and London, the *Sirius* was given a seventeen-gun salute, an honour never before given to a merchant ship. She did repeat the return voyage once more, but was never really intended for transatlantic routes, being far too small. Soon she returned to shorter runs and a calmer life.

It is difficult to write about the end of the *Sirius*. She really deserved better. She should have lived out her life peacefully, ending up cared for and treasured as a much-loved local icon. But less than a decade after that triumphant arrival in New York, she hit rocks off Ballycotton Bay in thick fog and was wrecked.

It was a cold and foggy January day in 1847, and the *Sirius* was coming down from Dublin to Cork with ninety crew and passengers. Striking one reef, she managed to refloat, but then came to grief on Smith's Rocks, half a mile from the port of Ballycotton, and began breaking up. A lifeboat was launched with twenty people on board, but it overturned and all in it were drowned.

> *… the steamer continued to thump heavily on the rocks, while the screams of alarm from the affrighted passengers, and the heavy surf breaking on her sides and on the deck rendered the scene one of awful danger and intense anxiety. Soon after the Coast Guard boat from Ballycotton Station, under command of Mr Coghlan, chief officer, came alongside, and the ship's boats having by this time been also launched, the remaining passengers were got into them and safely landed, though with the loss of every portion of their luggage, etc. We are sorry to learn that the country people in that wild and wretched locality availed themselves of the melancholy occasion to carry off everything they could lay their hands upon. Every article that was washed ashore, before the assistance of military or police arrived, was carried off by the people, who continued to assemble in large numbers …*

(Southern correspondent, *Belfast Commercial Chronicle*, Wednesday, 20 January 1847)

Among the goods that the local people regarded as claimable jetsam were groceries, musical instruments, books and furniture, as well as five cases of theatrical wardrobes belonging to a comedian of the Olympic Theatre, London. Presumably, he was travelling to fulfil a season in Cork. It is to be hoped that the good folk of Ballycotton made full use of these somewhat unorthodox garments.

More appropriately, the vital need for a lighthouse between the Old Head of Kinsale in Cork, and Hook Head in Waterford, was at last recognised. Work on the Ballycotton lighthouse began immediately, and it was first lit in 1851.

The shaft that drove the paddlewheel of the brave little steamer *Sirius* all the way to New York and back was rescued from Ballycotton. It now stands proudly on display by the waterside just outside Passage West, from whence the *Sirius* set sail on her historic voyage.

The Tsar approves …

As mentioned earlier, the steamship *Neptune* was launched from the Waterford shipyard that gave it its name in September 1849. Thousands of sightseers came from miles around to see the iron ship, the largest ever built in Ireland.

Long before six o clock vast crowds of people began to assemble, some betaking themselves of short excursions on the river, some taking up a select position on Cromwells Rock (Ferrybank side) and others resorting to the extensive yards of the Foundry … Our river, never surpassed in beauty, was thickly covered in shipping of all sorts, and from her majesty's steam ship Lucifer down to the humble cot, all bedecked on their gayest colours, which were fluttering in the breeze and

Ballycotton Lighthouse was built following the wreck of the *Sirius* there in 1847.

the delightful panoramic scene on the opposite shore can only be appreciated by those who had the happiness of witnessing it ... At six o clock all was intense anxiety, and a few minutes after, the fatal daggers were withdrawn, and while being christened Neptune *by the lady of John Malcomson, this beautiful monument of Irish industry glided magnificently into her 'native element' amid the most enthusiastic cheers, waving of handkerchiefs etc.*

(*Waterford News*, 21 September 1849)

Commissioned by the St Petersburg Steam Navigation Company for the route between that harbour and London, and clearly intended as a state-of-the-art showpiece, *Neptune* was subsequently fitted out in the most luxurious style. She made her maiden voyage from London to St Petersburg in 1849, where she was received with great pomp and circumstance by the city's mayor, who boarded the boat at Krondstadt for the final stretch up the River Neva.

As a final honour, the royal barge came down to meet her, the Tsar himself on board to view her stately lines. So impressed was His Imperial Majesty with her beauty that he announced she would not be liable for either pilot or port fees for the rest of her life. Unfortunately, that life was going to be shorter than anyone expected.

On her first return trip to London, *Neptune* carried the United States Minister to the Imperial Court, who was returning home to America, as well as some carefully packed Russian items for the Great Exhibition, a signal honour.

The Russian stand was to be one of the great attractions of that huge event organised by Prince Albert, and the goods carried by the *Neptune* were in all probability priceless, including as they did royal paintings, porcelain, fabrics and cut stone, among other treasures.

The Waterford-born ship brought them safely to London, and followed this up on her next trip with a second Russian treasure trove to be carefully unpacked in the Crystal Palace for the grand opening at the beginning of May 1851. Her place as one of the most elegant and luxurious ships to be found anywhere was now assured, and her creators at the shipyard must have felt proud.

Alas, it was not to be for long. Setting off for St Petersburg again in that same month, she ran aground near the Gulf of Finland and was wrecked. The many passengers on board were saved by the concerted efforts of the crew, and courageous boats from both the Swedish and the Finnish shores. They also managed to save her exceptionally valuable cargo, which included bales of expensive indigo and a large amount of bullion.

This first class splendid steam frigate known as the London and St Petersburg Steamship Neptune *has, we regret to say, been wrecked on a formidable reef in the Sound of Elsinore while pursuing a voyage from the Thames to the northern capital. It will be recollected she was specially selected to convey the numerous packages of Russian manufacture and produce for the Great Exhibition, which are now in the course of arrangement in the building, and having taken on board almost as valuable a cargo, was on her return voyage when the unfortunate accident befell her. It appears she left her moorings of Irongate Steam Wharf, St Katherine's, on the morning of the 27th ult, having on board about 40 passengers, a general cargo of merchandise, and some four or five carriages which were placed on deck. She made the Elsinore Light about half past ten o'clock on Sunday night last, the wind blowing rather fresh from the N.N.W., but beyond that there was no unfavourable circumstance. Nothing occurred to create the least alarm until she had steamed some 8 or 9 miles further, when suddenly she 'bounced' into a dangerous reef of rocks off that part of the coast called Swine Bottoms, off Logamass, and all was thrown into a state of consternation and dismay. The engines were backed, and every stratagem was resorted to to get her off, but without avail, the wind and rough sea acting on the vessel so as to drive her further into danger, and in less than half an hour the water had burst through her compartments (for she was an iron-built ship) and her hold was full up to within a foot of her main deck. Before this time attention was prudently directed towards saving the lives of the passengers, and the ship's signals being seen, several craft came alongside of the wreck. Some were landed on the Jutland coast and others on the opposite shore, Sweden. Vigorous efforts were made to save several bales of indigo, and other valuable portions of her cargo. In this the crew were successful. During the following day, owing to a heavy gale of wind, the ship sustained serious damage; so much so as to leave but little hope of her being got off. Her loss is much to be regretted. She was handsomely fitted up, and was a very fast steamer, having 250 horse power engines. From all accounts there appears to be no doubt that the ship was out of her course. Whether this arose through an error of judgement by those on board, or by some defect in her compass, which is probable, the vessel being built of iron, we have received no precise intelligence ... She was due at St Petersburg on the 4th. Another steamer has been placed on the station.*

(*Glasgow Sentinel*, 14 June 1851)

The Queen approves ...

The first iron-built ship from a Cork yard was the three-masted *Cormorant*, commissioned from Pikes' yard at Water Street by English purchasers:

On Saturday evening [9 April 1853] *the large iron screw-steamship* Cormorant *was launched from the yard of the Cork Steam Ship Company. This vessel is the largest which has as yet been built in this country; nearly the entire works have been executed at the factory of the Steam Ship Company. Her hull, masts, etc, are all of iron, wood being as little employed as possible. Her cabin is not, as usual, in the body of the vessel, but on deck, as commonly seen in American steamers. The ceremony of christening was performed by Miss Pike daughter of Mr. Ebez. Pike, of Besborough. The* Cormorant *is at present intended to ply between Liverpool and Rotterdam; the trade between which ports is greatly on the increase …*

(*Cork Constitution*)

Although originally intended for home use, the outbreak of the Crimean War necessitated a rapid adjustment in English maritime planning, and *Cormorant* was soon pressed into service transporting troops and equipment to that peninsula. While cavalry horses were being loaded at Portsmouth in May 1855, Queen Victoria and Prince Albert made a surprise visit from the Isle of Wight. Cue frantic preparations, swift tidying up and the hasty sourcing and laying of crimson carpets.

The screw steam-transport Cormorant *(No. 103), Capt. Byrne, was unexpectedly honoured this afternoon with a special royal visit; her Majesty wishing to see the manner in which her cavalry are berthed in their shipboard transit from England to the seat of war in the Crimea. According to all reports, the royal favour could not have been bestowed upon a more worthy ship than the* Cormorant, *which is one of the squadron of the Cork Screw Steamshipping Company …*

After inspecting the quarters where the horses were to spend the voyage, the royal couple looked around the deck, and were greatly taken by the ship's masts. Informed that they were built of iron, the Queen insisted on scraping them with the Prince Consort's penknife. Finding that they were indeed not of wood, she immediately ordered them to be recorded for use in the construction of masts for future Government ships then under construction in England. One can only wonder if, as the captain bowed royalty off the boat, a deck hand scurried hastily forward with a pot of paint …

The strange tale of the *Dei Gratia* and the *Mary Celeste*

Everyone has heard that weirdest of all sea stories, the *Mary Celeste* (the more familiar '*Marie Celeste*' was actually invented by Sir Arthur Conan Doyle for his novella on the inexplicable tale). Suggestions, solutions, conspiracy theories, radio programmes, television documentaries and literary works abound. What is not so well known, however, is that the boat that first discovered the ghost ship floating alone and empty, and towed her into a safe harbour, went on to have a busy later life operating out of Youghal in County Cork.

The story begins on 7 November 1872, when the sailing vessel *Mary Celeste* set out from New York, bound for Genoa in Italy. On board were Captain Benjamin Briggs, his wife and his two-year-old daughter, together with an experienced seven-man crew and a cargo of 1,700 barrels of industrial alcohol.

Twenty-eight days later, the sailing ship *Dei Gratia* was making its way down from Cobh (then called Queenstown) along the Spanish coast, when her crew spotted the *Mary Celeste*, adrift and abandoned. Its cargo was intact, there was food on the table, the stove was still burning, and a half-finished dress for the skipper's daughter lay on the bed in the cabin.

Captain Moorhouse of the *Dei Gratia* put some of his men on board and they took the boat to Gibraltar, where they rightfully claimed salvage. After a long and wearying case, where accusations, conspiracy theories and fierce arguments flew to and fro, they were eventually awarded the salvage, although, in a typically Dickensian touch, the costs of the inquiry took away most of that.

Lloyds List, March 31, 1873. The Mary Celeste. *In the Vice-Admiralty at Gibraltar on the 14th inst, the Hon. The Chief Justice gave judgement in the* Mary Celeste *salvage case, and awarded the sum of £1,700 to the*

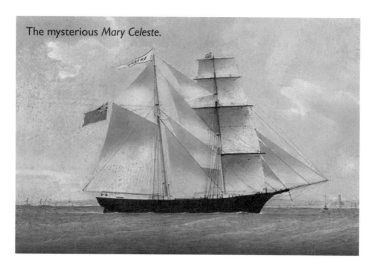

The mysterious *Mary Celeste*.

master and crew of the Nova Scotian brigantine Dei
Gratia *for the salvage services rendered by them; the
costs of the suit to be paid out of the property salved …*

Perhaps the protracted arguments, and the many accusations
levelled at the *Dei Gratia*, made her owners feel she was an
unlucky ship, because in 1881 they sold her to a successful
businessman and ship owner in Youghal, County Cork, one
Martin Fleming.

Mr Fleming immediately put her to active use, bringing
coal across from Wales. She worked this route for twenty-five
years. Once or twice she seems to have ventured considerably
further afield, as in 1887, when she somehow ended up in
New Brunswick in need of repairs:

*Lloyds List, Aug 30, 1887. St John, N.B., Aug 15. The
Port Wardens have held a survey on brig* Dei Gratia,
*Youghal, and recommended that the foremast be taken
out, rudder head, check and rail repaired, and other
damage made good.*

The phrasing suggests that the port was at fault rather than
the feisty little brigantine. Perhaps she was paying a visit
to the shipyard in nearby Nova Scotia where she was born?
Unfortunately we will never know.

In 1907, fate caught up with the *Dei Gratia*. Sheltering
from a December gale in Milford Haven, she slipped her
moorings and was blown onto a dangerous reef known as
Blackrock near Dale. Here she lay, suffering more and more

damage from the wind and waves, as the local Lloyds agent worriedly indicated in a flurry of telegrams to his head office:

1. Sent steam trawler to her assistance.

2. Sent steamer down this morning to tow her off; not successful. If not successful tonight's tide, will go down early morning and wire you from Dale.

3. Re Dei Gratia: *Full of water last night, badly holed, deck breaking up. Fear total loss. Will remain here till I can inspect her at low water. Vessel lying against rocks.*

Although that is as far as the records go on the UK side of the water, the story continues on the Irish side. The *Dei Gratia* was apparently towed back to her home base by the Fleming company and then became, somewhat ignobly, a coal hulk at the quays in Cobh. Today, the remains of the boat that discovered the *Mary Celeste* are said to lie under the piers of Haulbowline Island, close by. What story could she tell of that strange sea mystery; what unrevealed secrets does she hold to herself under those dark lapping waters?

Never lost a life

Kept till last is the heart-warming story of the *Jeanie Johnston*, a truly noble ship that carried thousands of emigrants from Kerry to the New World during the Famine, and never suffered a single life to be lost throughout her sturdy career. To her final moments, she kept firmly to that principle.

So honoured is her memory in Ireland's emigration history that a reproduction was built in the 1990s, which repeated many of the voyages she made across the Atlantic. That new *Jeanie Johnston*, when not acting as a sail training vessel, moors on Dublin's quays, where she operates as a floating living history museum, telling the story of the Famine and emigration.

She is not the only replica of a famine ship: the *Dunbrody* at New Ross was similarly rebuilt to honour that vessel's history. The *Dunbrody* also lies moored there on the Barrow as a historic site to visit, but the life of the *Jeanie Johnston* has aspects which make it unique.

The original *Jeanie Johnston*, a three-masted sailing barque, was built in Quebec in 1847, and bought by the Tralee-based timber merchants John O'Donovan and Sons. She traded between those two ports for many years, taking people out and bringing timber back. Departing emigrants crowded to the quayside in Blennerville, next to the huge windmill erected by the Blennerhassett family.

Although it is now overgrown and almost forgotten, you can still find that old quayside today, and think of the many folk – men, women, children, some weeping, some excited, many apprehensive – who gathered here, gazing up at the tall masts of the ship that was to take them to the New World.

The voyage, which cost somewhere between £3 and £5, took on average about forty-seven days. In sharp contrast to the many appalling stories of 'coffin ships' and emigrant deaths (over 5,000 are known to have died at sea, and over 5,000 buried on Grosse Isle, on the Quebec route, alone),

The mill and quayside at Blennerville where emigrants embarked on the *Jeanie Johnston*.

during the seven years it operated out of Tralee, the *Jeanie Johnston* is renowned for never having lost a single life on board, either of crew or passenger. It seems that the owners were careful in providing for the good health of everyone on the ship, even to the extent of putting a doctor on each run.

On its very first voyage, indeed, the number of passengers was unexpectedly increased by one, before the vessel had even quitted Tralee:

> *The Messrs Donovan's beautiful barque, the* Jeanie Johnston *of Tralee, James Attridge master, sailed from our port on the morning of Monday the 24th inst, with about 22 emigrants for Quebec. Very great satisfaction was expressed by the emigrants, who were for the most part strong farmers and artisans with their families, at the general comfort presented on board. Indeed the friends of the emigrants who had visited them ere they sped on their watery*

course, speak with an affectionate enthusiasm of the paternal care paid by the Messrs Donovan to every passenger. The day after all the passengers were on board, and the barque ready for sea, a fine young woman, daughter to a respectable farmer near this town, Mr Thomas Foran, and wife to Daniel Ryal, gave birth to a very fine male child. Thanks to the prompt and skilful attendance of Dr. Richard Blennerhassett of Tralee, who went out as Surgeon to the ship, the mother and child left our port in perfect health. The Rev. Mr Moore RCC of Ardfert baptized the child on the following day, and the passengers and parents, to mark their feelings to the owners for their care, not only on this occasion, but for the entire outfit of the ship, and their anxiety for the comfort of the passengers in general, called the child after the principal owner and the ship, viz Nicholas Johnston Ryal.

(*Tralee Chronicle*, Saturday, 29 April 1848)

A very good start, and so it continued. A typical newspaper report is that of the *Kerry Evening Post* of 26 May 1849, which records:

It affords us much pleasure to have to announce the safe arrival on the 3rd inst of the barque Jeanie Johnston, *James Attridge master, at Baltimore, United States, where she landed all her passengers in good health …*

In 1855, after a praiseworthy career as the safest emigrant ship known, *Jeanie Johnston* was sold to a William Johnson in England, who operated it on a similar timber run. In October 1858, en route from Quebec to Hull, she encountered stormy weather and her heavy load became dangerously waterlogged. The captain, his wife, their child and the crew suffered ten days of abject terror, struggling against the sea in a fight for survival.

We sailed from Quebec at daylight on the morning of October 5 (deals) for Hull. Our crew consisted of 11 men, my mate, and myself, besides my wife and child, a little boy two years old, making altogether 15 of us. We went on well with moderate breezes until the evening of the 21st at eleven o'clock, when it came on to blow from the N.N.E. rather freshly ...

The gale increased, and we discovered that the ship was making water very fast ... At 5am we shipped a heavy sea, which washed away our quarter-boats and davits, and swept away small articles overboard. The gale continued unabated until 1.40pm when we were boarded by another heavy sea, which washed away the cabin skylight, the binnacle, etc, and stove in the top of the cabin. The gale continued in full force till 9.30pm of the same day, when a third monstrous sea struck the ship, which stove in the front of the cabin, which was a house on deck, filling it with water, and washing everything in the starboard side of it overboard. It also washed away the long boat and jolly boat. At 11.40pm the ship was full of water and the pumps were of no further use. The ship's bulwarks were nearly all washed away, and the sea made a clean breach over her. All hands now determined to take to the main rigging, as they did not know the moment the ship might go down. My wife was in bed in the cabin with her child, and I came to her and told her that 'we must all take to the main rigging.' She was very much affected by this news, but said she would go. So great was the danger that she had no time to put any clothes on her scarcely, with the exception of a coat and one or two other loose garments ...

We gathered up what bread we could, and tried to get some fresh water, but found that all the casks had been washed overboard. We secured ourselves in the maintop with canvas and ropes ... At seven o'clock the next morning, we saw a sail to leeward; she was also a barque and passed within about a mile of us. We were in continual danger, expecting the mainmast to go over the ship's side. Our clothes were wet. We could not stretch ourselves, but were all huddled together without room to stir. My child was quiet, sometimes slept a little and occasionally cried for a drink which he could not get. On the 23rd we all began to feel the want of fresh water. On the 24th, at noon, we saw a brig to leeward of us pass to the westward; she did not notice us ...

(*Hull Packet*, 31 December 1858)

175

The new *Jeanie Johnston*,
moored at Cork quays.

Eventually, after ten terrible days, barely surviving on rain water in the rigging, the boat sinking lower and lower into the ocean, a Dutch ship, the *Sophie Elizabeth*, saw what pitiful signals of distress they were still able to wave and came alongside to rescue them. Then, and only then, having seen her passengers safely away, did the *Jeanie Johnston* let herself slip quietly below the waves. Her final task was done, and her unspotted record remained.

Small wonder then that the idea of rebuilding this paragon among ships should have taken hold in Ireland, where such inspiring records are sadly few from those Famine days. The new *Jeanie Johnston* was built at Blennerville, which was considered rightly to be the only place the massive project should be carried out.

Over 300 shipwrights and craftsmen worked determinedly on her for six years. Completed in 2002, she retraced several of those historic voyages of her ancestor, visiting many large American ports. Some of the 10,000 eager onlookers who witnessed her emerging from the mists in Baltimore harbour in the early morning, or saw her come safely to rest in New York, confess to weeping as they saw history repeat itself. After all, many of their own family members might have emigrated in just such a boat. Long may the new *Jeanie Johnston* uphold the superb standard set by her predecessor.

Hook Head Lighthouse, one of the oldest in the world still operating.

CHAPTER V

Storms and Shipwrecks

IN WHAT QUARTER STANDS THE WIND?

For anyone living in close proximity to the sea, the ability to read every signal given by the weather – wind direction, darkening skies, unusual stillness – is learned from childhood. Away from the coast, most of us rely on television news for advance warning of storms, while yachtsmen keep their ears sharply tuned to the shipping forecast. More and more, we are losing the skill of eyeing those clouds, sniffing the breeze, noticing what animals and birds are doing as they sense approaching trouble.

Back in the old days, coastal dwellers and onshore fishermen had their weather skills honed to the sharpest possible degree. The day's activities were dictated by the currents of air, the look of the skies. The captains of merchant ships that sailed further, to far-off shores, were well acquainted with the trade winds and when the best time was to travel east or west.

Even so, fisherman or foreign traveller, all could be taken by surprise. A sudden change in wind direction could drive a vessel, hitherto proceeding smoothly, onto a rocky shore and disaster. A small craft moored as safely as possible in harbour could be torn from its anchorage, bringing ruin to a small family that depended on it for their living. A calm and wind-less morning gives no guarantee that a howling storm will not blow up before evening. And where the wind leads, the sea follows, always ready to respond, the millpond becoming the maelstrom in the wink of an eye. The Irish coast has a well-deserved reputation for untrustworthiness.

Even in ancient times, our old legends show that everyone knew of particular parts of the coast where the sea was most unfriendly. As part of their fate, the Children of Lir are con-demned to 300 years as swans on the notorious Sea of Moyle, between the north of Ireland and Scotland, and there are heartrending descriptions of all four swan children huddled on a rock in the dashing waves of winter, Fionnuala wrap-ping her wings around her three brothers to hold them safely together.

A graceful sculpture of the Children stands today, facing that sea on the quayside at Ballycastle.

In 440 AD, Breacain, grandson of Niall of the Nine Hostages, perished with all the goods and cattle he was trading to Scotland,

At Ballycastle on the Antrim coast, the Children of Lir fly together for ever.

having miscalculated the tides in these treacherous waters. A few centuries later, a medieval monk wrote in the margin of a text he was inscribing:

> *Fierce is the wind tonight,*
> *It tosses the ocean's white hair,*
> *Tonight I fear not the Danish invader,*
> *Coasting on the Irish sea ...*

Storms at sea and on shore were to influence the course of history in centuries to come, attacking the powerful as well as the poor. Armies and merchants, sailors and fishermen, city dwellers and farmers – nature treated them all with the same casual disregard.

The Spanish Armada

In the autumn of 1588, King Philip II of Spain sent a gigantic fleet, 130 strong, to invade and conquer England. He could not have envisaged the appalling fate that would overtake so many of his men and their ships off the west coast of Ireland. At that time, Spain was probably the most powerful country in the world, while England was doing its best to overtake it. The invasion, reasoned Philip, would settle once and for all who was in charge. How could he know that wild weather would change the path of history so completely?

The Spanish galleons suffered much damage in naval battles with the English defenders under Lord Charles Howard and Sir Francis Drake, but their problems were multiplied when fierce storm winds began to blow up, driving them north-ward. The crews began to run dangerously low on supplies of ammunition and food. Urgent meetings were held among the commanders. The admiral of the Spanish fleet, Medina Sidonia, decided that the best thing was to return home while they were still able so to do. He issued surprisingly precise instructions, given the difficult circumstances in which they found themselves:

> *The course that is first to be held is to the north/north-east until you be found under 61 degrees and a half;* **and then to take great heed lest you fall upon the Island of Ireland for fear of the harm that may happen unto you upon that coast** [my emphasis]. *Then, parting from those islands and doubling the Cape in 61 degrees and a half, you shall run west/south-west until you be found*

under 58 degrees; and from thence to the south-west to
the height of 53 degrees; and then to the south/south-
west, making to the Cape Finisterre, and so to procure
your entrance into The Groyne A Coruña or to Ferrol, or
to any other port of the coast of Galicia.

It was good guidance, essentially a great anti-clockwise cir-
cuit of Britain and Ireland, but it was almost impossible to
follow, given the atrocious weather conditions and the lack of
advanced navigational equipment. The Clerk of the Weather,
sitting far above in the skies, rubbed his hands and decided to
stir things up – with catastrophic results. Storms continued
with increasing ferocity while the ships desperately endeavoured to keep clear of the Irish coast. All to no avail. Strong
south-westerly gales – which occur all too frequently today, as
coastal dwellers well know – now came into the picture. One
can only sympathise with the beleaguered captain who wrote,
'We sailed without knowing whither through constant fogs,
storms and squalls.'

From Antrim in the north right down to Kerry in the
south, some twenty-four ships of the Armada were driven on
to the rocky coastline and totally wrecked. Some of the poor
exhausted Spaniards managed to swim or struggle ashore, but
the reception they received was, sadly, not what they would
have hoped for. The English Crown had every reason to dis-
trust Spain, and had issued ironclad orders that survivors
were to be put to death immediately. If any Irish, they added
viciously, were found to have rescued or assisted them in any
way, they would be tortured and put to death themselves.

One supposes that England had a right to its point of view, seeing that this was a matter of war, but it is desperately sad to think of those salt-sodden mariners crawling ashore, choking and gasping, grateful to reach dry land – only to be seized by brutal hands and to feel cold steel at their throats. And it is perhaps understandable that Irish landowners, fearful for their own lives and those of their families, felt that they had no option but to obey and kill these few unhappy survivors.

Among the peasantry though, as well as one or two proud chieftains who refused to bend the knee to Elizabeth's command, sympathy was not wanting, and some hundred Spaniards did survive to get back to Spain. A few indeed remained in Ireland, bequeathing their dark hair and flashing eyes to many generations of the families who sheltered them in fearful secrecy. One man, Francisco De Cuellar, managed to survive by following a dangerous and exhausting route that led him all the way across Ireland to Scotland, and on to the Spanish Netherlands, from where he could finally get home. Today, as some recompense for this tragic episode, several monuments have been raised to the memory of those ill-fated sailors along the western coastline of Ireland.

One Armada commander, Juan Martinez de Recalde, was fortunate in already having some knowledge of the Irish coast. By seizing a small Scottish fishing boat in the strait between Ireland and Scotland, and persuading its crew to assist in guiding them, he managed to bring the *San Juan de Bautista* all the way south and safely to shelter among the Blasket Islands off Kerry. Here he had to remain for some

A memorial to the ill-fated Spanish Armada, at Spanish Point in Co. Clare.

A striking mural depicting the Armada, on a building in Grange, Co. Sligo.

time, while the weather continued wild and Crown forces massed on the mainland to seize the ship and crew if they dared venture ashore. In the end, the winds relented, and de Recalde was able to sail home.

He was one of very few. Only some sixty of the original 130 ships of the proud Armada returned to Spain, and it is estimated that some 15,000 Spaniards lost their lives in the ill-fated attempt on England. It could have turned out so very differently. But that's the way with the weather. You cannot count on it doing what you want.

The French expedition of 1796

Ireland's wild weather and dangerous coastal waters thwarted another attempted attack on England over 200 years later. The Society of United Irishmen, led by Theobald Wolfe Tone, had persuaded a force of the First French Republic to come over and assist them in their fight to drive the British out of Ireland. For their part, the French saw it as a first step to an invasion of England itself, and were very willing to cooperate. A force of around 15,000 soldiers gathered at Brest in December of 1796, and set out for Ireland.

Unfortunately, one of the stormiest winters of the eighteenth century had been chosen for the attack, with the French fleet completely unprepared for the conditions they met. The fleet was blown in several directions, and while most of the boats did manage to reach the rendezvous point off Mizen Head, its commanders were driven miles further on into the

A hazardous meeting place for the French fleet: Mizen Head in Co. Cork.

An anchor from a French ship, now displayed in Bantry.

Atlantic by fierce easterly headwinds. This left the main body of the attacking force without any orders to proceed to the landing point at Bantry Bay. Within a week, French boats were making their way back to Brest through storms, fog and the unwelcome attentions of British patrols.

The weather was somewhat better in 1798, and French soldiers managed to land at Killala Bay. They then marched halfway across Ireland before being surrounded and defeated by British troops. Wolfe Tone was captured, and committed suicide in prison before the Crown could carry out the brutal ceremonial execution they had planned for him.

A light in the darkness

Lighthouses have for many centuries been a vital aid to those struggling through bad weather at sea. In some particularly

Hook Head lighthouse has guided seafarers for centuries.

dangerous parts of our coast, beacons or other warning lights were in existence long before improved technology made the building of permanent lighthouses a possibility. Hook Head, which stands at the tip of the peninsula of that name in Wexford, guarding the entrance to Waterford Harbour, is one of the oldest in the world. It is the second oldest lighthouse still operating, after the Tower of Hercules in northern Spain (from where, in all probability, the Celts set sail on their voyage to claim Ireland in ancient times).

A monk called Dubhán is said to have set up a beacon here in the fifth century, but the current tower dates from the twelfth or early thirteenth, being constructed under the orders of William Marshall, Strongbow's son-in-law. Strongbow himself landed not far from here on that first Norman invasion of Ireland in 1170, so he would have had good cause to remember that treacherous coastline. The monks of a nearby monastery (in all probability that founded by Dubhán) were the first keepers of the all-important light that had to be kept burning at night.

By the nineteenth century, with improved communications and technology, there were lighthouses all around the Irish coast, some of them in what seem like the most impossibly inaccessible places, such as the Bull Rock off Kerry, or the Fastnet off West Cork, where the mind boggles at how they got the cut stone there in the first place, let alone struggled up the sheer rock faces with it and put the buildings together. But the tenacity of those lighthouse builders has saved many a ship from loss.

The wreck of the *Seahorse* off Tramore in 1816, with appalling loss of life, led to the construction of a most unusual additional visual beacon to aid navigation. This was nothing less than a gigantic metal man, brightly painted and dressed in a sailor's attire, which still stands at the entrance to Waterford Harbour.

The Fastnet lighthouse.

The *Seahorse*, originally a fighting three-master commanded by Horatio Nelson, was used as a transport ship in its later years. On that January night in 1816, en route from Ramsgate to Cork, it was heavily overcrowded with soldiers, their wives and their children, as well as crew and officers. Increasing gales, and the unfortunate death by falling from the rigging of the only local sailor who knew the coastline, meant the captain had to rely on seeing the signal of a lighthouse to find his way safely to harbour. By dawn the lookout could glimpse Hook Head, outside Wexford, but the storm relentlessly drove the battered ship southward. Around noon, the *Seahorse* made her fatal mistake and entered Tramore Bay rather than Waterford Harbour. Waterford offers a huge and safe anchorage, while Tramore most definitely does not, and the ship struck rocks almost immediately.

Although they were less than a mile from shore, neither the ship nor its passengers had a chance. The *Seahorse* broke in half and sank, with helpless onlookers on the beach unable to launch boats to help the unfortunates who were swept to their doom. Some brave rescuers waded into the raging sea to drag in anybody who came within reach.

Of the 393 on board, only thirty were saved, all men, who presumably had the strength to swim some distance. The women, clutching their children desperately, had little chance. There is a monument to the tragedy on the waterfront at Tramore, and the peaceful graveyard at Drumcannon marks the last resting place of those lost.

It was decided that such a thing should never be allowed to happen again, if it could be prevented, and steps were

The peaceful graveyard at Drumcannon, Co. Waterford, where those lost in the *Seahorse* tragedy now lie at rest.

immediately taken to ensure that no ship could mistake the entrance to Waterford Harbour and safety in future.

Huge pillars, each over sixty feet high, were placed in strategic spots in 1823: two at Brownstown Head, and three at Great Newtown Head, all funded by Lloyds of London. These were, and still are, clear navigational markers, which could be counted down: three at Great Newtown first, then the two at Brownstown, which led to a single pillar at Hook Head. Then, as a final touch, the fourteen-foot metal man was placed on the central pillar at Great Newtown Head, his right arm pointing towards the sea and indicating the safe route to follow.

Designed by Thomas Kirk, a noted English sculptor, he is kept freshly repainted and is a stirring feature suddenly to catch sight of, either from the cliffs or from out at sea today. Local legend holds that on stormy nights he calls out a warning to passing ships. And the town of Tramore does not forget

The Metal Man on his tall pillar on the Waterford coast.

The Metal Man at Rosses Point in Sligo.

the tragedy. The Sea Horse Tavern at number 3 Strand Street commemorates one of Ireland's worst maritime disasters.

You can find the fellow to the Metal Man at Brownstown Head up in Sligo, at Rosses Point, marking the entrance to the town harbour. He stands on a fifteen-foot tower over the Perch Rock by Oyster Island, which, prior to his arrival, was the cause of many shipwrecks.

He now boasts a flashing light as well, to aid navigation in the dark, and has been said to terrify many a look-out on a foreign ship by suddenly looming gigantically out of the mist at night.

Wild weather doesn't just affect ships at sea, of course. It can bring disaster and sudden death along the coast at any time without warning. Extreme conditions in Dublin Bay in the winter of 1763 sank the quarantine sloop (used to hold arrivals suspected of carrying disease); drove a barge hosting a lively entertainment on the rocks at Dún Laoghaire (happily they were all taken off safely by a friendly coal boat); and sank a pleasure boat on a fishing trip beyond Bullock Harbour, with the loss of all on board. All around the coast, at any time of year, the same kind of events are reported: sudden bad weather, small boats sunk, larger vessels run aground or wrecked, often loss of life, tragedy.

There is a strange story concerning the only survivor of a ship called the *Anne and Mary*, which was wrecked on the coast of Kerry in 1859. Michael McDaniel finally made it home to New Ross the following February to tell the tale. It appears that he and eight others set out from Trondheim in Norway the previous September with a cargo of deal planks, and found themselves in early October fairly close to the Aran Islands.

Thinking it was now safe to anchor and take rest, they did so; but almost immediately a squall hit, and the boat was overturned. They eventually managed to right her by cutting away the rigging and most of the masts; but with the squall increasing to a storm, their entire cabin, with all their provisions and navigational equipment, was swept away.

For ten days they were tossed about, with no way of steering or indeed making any headway, and with no food whatsoever, except for two rats that they managed to catch. These, Mr McDaniel stresses, were shared out fairly among the starving crew. Unfortunately, we do not know what happened to his eight fellow sufferers. Perhaps it is as well that we do not.

In West Cork in 1894, a violent storm brought chaos to the harbour of Baltimore, as a newspaper reported:

During today and since ten o'clock last night, a violent storm has been raging along this coast, doing serious damage ... it is on sea that all the havoc is being wrought, and it is feared that many a poor fisherman and mariner have perished ... Many boats are missing, and a good deal of floating wreckage is observable outside Baltimore Harbour. An ice hulk has gone to pieces on the rocks in the bay, and a French smack had a very narrow escape of a similar fate ... This evening a full-rigged barque was seen flying a flag of distress outside Baltimore Harbour, and a crew of Islanders proceeded to the rescue. The barque proved to be the Norwegian barque Christiana Wilhelm, *from Port Talbot to New Brunswick. She had a crew of some dozen hands, including the captain, all of whom were safely rescued. The barque has completely disappeared and is fast breaking up. None of the effects could be saved in the raging storm, which still continues to increase rather than abate. Another Norwegian barque was driven into Castletownshend harbour in a most disabled state, being totally dismasted and having only one mast standing, but the crew was safe. The Manx fishing lugger, number 23, and hailing from Port St. Mary, arrived here at 4 o'clock this evening with her rails washed away, and the skipper, whose name is Kirk or Quirk, washed overboard and drowned. The rails and small boats of the fishing smack* Florence, *of Kilkeel, County Down, were washed in at Trafaska,*

*near here, also, this evening, and it is feared that
the smack and crew of eight are lost.* The Pride of
Sherkin, *fishing vessel, is also missing, and grave
apprehensions exist regarding her safety.*

Oiche na Gaoithe Móra:
The Night of the Big Wind

This terrifying night in 1839 has become part of our folk
tradition, never forgotten, cropping up again and again in
literature, used as a comparison in times of storm, and used
as a byword for apocalyptic events.

The totally unexpected windstorm or hurricane swept
across Ireland from west to east on 6 January 1839, leaving a
trail of wreckage and disaster behind it. The worst storm to
hit the country for 300 years, it brought gusts of 185km an
hour (115mph). First felt on the west coast in Mayo, it moved
very slowly across Ireland throughout the day, gathering even

The Night of the Big Wind brought terror and wreckage all over Ireland.

more strength as it went. The seas rose frighteningly. Waves even topped the 700-foot Cliffs of Moher.

By midnight, it had reached hurricane force, and the damage everywhere was terrible. Up to 300 people lost their lives, and at least forty-two ships were wrecked. Storm surges drew the sea inland, causing serious flooding to villages and hamlets, where many simple cottages had already been wrecked, taking even the most basic shelter away from their terrified inhabitants.

Many thought the end of the world had come. A particularly gruesome side effect saw coffins rising from their graves when the trees surrounding them in churchyards were uprooted.

Everywhere, great stands of ancient trees were knocked down, churches and venerable buildings reduced to rubble; even Ballybunion Castle in Kerry, which had stood proudly for so long, defying the centuries, was brought to earth. Salt brine coated bushes and hedgerows in the very centre of the country, while stocks of hay and corn were destroyed, resulting in starvation for surviving livestock in the months that followed.

Dublin, being on the east coast, escaped the worst of the hurricane, but considerable damage was done to houses, with roofs being ripped off and chimneys smashing into the street. People huddled in the safest corners they could find, waiting for daylight. The *Freeman's Journal* painted a graphic picture:

> *The storm with which this city was visited on Sunday night was one of the most violent which has blown from the face of Heaven within the memory of the oldest inhabitants ... Not a soul dare venture into the streets; the lamps were, almost without any exception, extinguished; and amidst the roaring of the hurricane,*

which threatened to sweep every obstacle before it from the surface of the earth, the pealing of fire-bells – the sounds of falling chimneys – windows breaking and slates and tiles flying through the streets, were fearfully audible; and sometimes the still more dreadful shrieks of the alarmed inmates of the tottering houses reached the ear; while the rocking walls and falling walls threatened them momentarily with destruction … At intervals dense clouds obscured the sky, and added to the horror of the scene by the gloomy darkness which they produced; but when they were driven by, the heavens did not appear less ominous; for the Aurora Borealis burned brightly a great portion of the night, mantling the hemisphere with sheets of red, and corresponding well with the lurid gleams which ascended to the zenith from the flames of burning houses that the tempest threatened to fan into a general conflagration.

Two ships out of Belfast, the *Ann* and the *Juno*, were lost with all hands; in Donegal, several families were buried beneath the ruins of their homes. In Sligo, fishing boats were smashed at their moorings; six cargo ships laden with grain, which had left early on the Sunday morning, just before the storm struck, disappeared without trace; the bodies of fourteen men were washed ashore the day after the storm.

In Scattery Roads, at the mouth of the Shannon, the schooner *Undine*, belonging to the Limerick Shipping Company, was riding out the storm at anchor, when a brig named the *John of Leith* came drifting by, dragging her anchors and seeming all too likely to run the *Undine* down. The captain of the *Undine* had no option but to lift his own anchors and move out of the other boat's path, but his ship was swept on to the rocks at Moyne, where she was wrecked. Two of the hands were swept overboard; the bodies of the captain and a crew member were discovered on the deck next day, having apparently died of exhaustion and exposure.

Three young boys on the brig *Grecian*, out of Hull, were more fortunate – when their ship ran aground at Kilrush, they clung to the rigging until morning, when they were rescued.

Poor people were of course most affected by the damage wrought, their small and insecure homes being either completely wrecked or rendered uninhabitable with the roofs torn off. What must it have been like, in the freezing dawn of a January day, after a night of terror, to find yourself without a home, a fire, or any of the things that make life bearable or even liveable?

That terrifying night became enfolded in Irish legend ever after. In fact, when pensions were introduced in 1908 for those over seventy (many of whom would be unable to furnish certificates of age), one of the queries used to establish qualification was whether the applicant remembered the Night of the Big Wind.

The *Northern Whig* summed it up thus:

> *Every part of Ireland – every field, every town, every village – has felt its dire effects, from Galway to Dublin, from the Giant's Causeway to the Island of Valentia. It has been, we repeat it, the most awful, the most extraordinary calamity of the kind, with which the people were ever afflicted …*

The Old Head of Kinsale in Co. Cork.

The *City of Chicago*

One of the most exciting shipwrecks to have occurred (that is, from the point of view of newsworthiness) was that of the liner *City of Chicago*. En route from New York to Liverpool, she ran onto the rocks at the Old Head of Kinsale in County Cork on 1 July 1892. The interest occurs not so much in the fact of a large passenger vessel being stranded, but in the location, and also in the highly dramatic way in which the passengers were rescued.

The Old Head has been since earliest times a very definite landmark on the West Cork coast. Standing out a considerable distance from the mainland, it housed a beacon to guide ships from medieval times, with a lighthouse in situ since the seventeenth century. It rises 200 feet from the sea, with beetling cliffs that are quite dangerous for the unwary scrambler. Looking down from the top is frightening enough; to look up from below gives rise to a swimming sense of dizziness.

Yet that is just what the unfortunate passengers of the *City of Chicago* found themselves doing on that dark and foggy night. Earlier in the day, they had passed Brow Head, the southernmost tip of Ireland, and later Cape Clear. Those intending to disembark at Cork were thinking of getting their baggage together, when suddenly the lookout shouted frantically, 'Breakers ahead!'

Almost instantly, the steamer ground onto a reef of vicious rocks, and her bow ran right into a large cave. Distress rockets were immediately fired, and then the captain ordered the lifeboats to be launched rather than wait for help to come, which might take too long. From the lifeboats, people were put on to a narrow stretch of beach and flat rocks, which of course would only stay dry until the tide turned.

The residents of the Old Head knew the sea, and realised that there was a serious emergency in progress. From all sides,

The wreck of the *City of Chicago* at the Old Head of Kinsale in 1892.

carrying ropes, they rushed from their cottages and made for the tip of the headland. With great courage, some of them swarmed down the dangerous cliff to a rocky ledge from where a rope could be thrown. By this means, over 100 frightened passengers were hauled up, and then guided onwards by additional ropes to the very top of the cliff and comparative safety.

Now the Kinsale coastguards arrived, bringing rope ladders with wooden rungs. These were unrolled over the cliff, and the rest of the passengers climbed up, trembling in fear. Remember that this was the late Victorian age, and the ladies on board this fine ship would have been dressed in their best and most voluminous gowns. It could hardly have been an easy task to climb a swaying rope ladder up such a terrifying cliff. However, the alternative was hardly attractive, and so they discovered strengths they never knew they had, holding their nerve and grasping the ladder with firm hands.

There was almost a tragedy. A young mother was climbing with her baby somehow clutched in one arm, while the other grasped the ladder. The child wriggled and fell from her hold. With lightning reflexes, a sailor on the rocks below saw the incident and caught the baby as it fell, calling up a reassurance to its frantic parent. The reunion at the top of the cliff must have been a thankful one.

But there was still a long way to go before the warmth, food and hot drinks that were so desperately needed could be obtained. On a dark and foggy night, over hillocks and hollows, tearing their clothes on gorse bushes and stubbing their feet against stones, the passengers made their way to

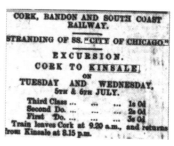

various cottages on the Head, which were thrown open for their comfort. Some made use of the coastguard tenders and were taken on to Kinsale. No-one was lost.

One man complained afterwards that he had been over-charged for food and for a charter boat to return to the wreck to rescue his luggage, but he was the exception. The rest were grateful to their rescuers – indeed, grateful to be alive. And the Cork, Bandon and South Coast Railway was quick to organise excursion trains to Kinsale, so that sightseers could view the wreck for themselves.

The *Titanic* **and the** *Lusitania*

In many ways the fate of these two great ships, one of the White Star and one of the Cunard Line, are not part of our story, since the first met its end off Newfoundland, and the second was torpedoed during wartime rather than being wrecked by storms, but both have very strong links with the town of Cobh, and their demand to be included here could not go unheard.

The RMS *Titanic* was of course built by Harland & Wolff in Belfast. On her triumphant maiden voyage from Southampton to New York, the luxury liner made one final call to Cobh to disembark some short-haul passengers and take on those who were waiting to travel on to America. So large was this leviathan that she could not possibly come right into Cobh, instead mooring grandiloquently out in the wider reaches of

Cork Harbour, by Roches Point lighthouse, with tenders ferrying passengers on and off. Eight left the ship, while 123 boarded: three heading for first class, seven for second class, and the remaining 113 to the less comfortable but far less expensive steerage section. At least thirty-two of those steerage passengers were Irish-born emigrants, hoping to make a future in the New World.

In total, this splendid ship was carrying 2,223 passengers and crew when she set sail from Cork. Only 712 were saved from the disaster after she crashed into an iceberg in the early hours of 15 April 1912, with those below decks in steerage having far less chance of survival than the well-to-do on the upper decks.

One Irishwoman who did escape was Violet Jessop, who was a stewardess on board. A nineteen-year-old lad from Longford named Thomas McCormack also survived, by jumping

The ill-fated *Titanic*.

The White Star pier in Cobh, from which so many emigrated to the New World.

into the icy waters and then swimming desperately from one crammed lifeboat to another until some women took pity on him and pulled him in.

A Jeremiah Burke from Glanmire was not so fortunate. In his last moments on board the ill-fated ship, he scribbled a note, thrust it into a bottle, corked it and threw it overboard. It is said to have been washed up on the shore hardly a mile from his native home. It read simply: 'From Titanic. Good bye all. Burke of Glanmire, Cork.'

Today, the former White Star Line office on the waterfront in Cobh is a much-visited tourist attraction. Outside, the dilapidated pier, from which tenders took passengers out to the massive ship over a century ago, can still be seen.

In New York, Pier 59, where the *Titanic* was due to arrive to a traditional fanfare, also still stands, battered and empty, but all the more haunting for that. Survivors who had been picked up by the *Carpathia* in 1912 were brought instead to nearby Pier 54, where thousands of drawn-faced and anxious people waited for news of their loved ones.

Strangely enough, that same Pier 54 in New York was the one from which the Cunard Line's *Lusitania* set off three years later, headed for Liverpool. Despite strong warnings from the German Embassy in New York that it was extremely inadvisable to make the voyage, she nevertheless went ahead on 1 May, with 1,959 passengers and crew. On 7 May, she was torpedoed by a U-boat 18km (11 miles) off the Old Head of Kinsale. Onlookers on the cliffs watched in horror as she sank almost immediately.

Efforts were instantly underway to instigate rescue, and small craft put out from several harbours to do what they could.

A model of the *Lusitania* at Courtmacsherry, Co. Cork.

A monument to the *Lusitania* in Cobh.

The Courtmacsherry lifeboat was one of the first to respond, its crew rowing valiantly out from Barry's Point to pick up survivors.

Tragically, since 1,198 people were drowned and just 761 survived, all too many bodies were brought ashore in Cobh for attempts at identification and eventual reverential burial. Today, an impressive sculpture stands in the centre of the town commemorating that event, and an old graveyard up on the hills behind is the last resting place of those passengers who lost their lives.

The graveyard above Cobh where many of those drowned are buried.

Deep sea caves have always been ideal for smugglers.

CHAPTER VI

No Moon Tonight: The Smuggling Game

Of course, the gentlemen who practised this risky commercial enterprise around the Irish coast scorned the title 'smuggling', opting instead for the term 'free trading'. It was trying enough to have England firmly ruling the roost on our island, they might explain (although only to very trusted friends), but when crippling tariffs were imposed on goods both going out and coming in, that was the final straw.

Wool, one of our largest exports since very early times, and for which the weavers of France and Flanders were crying out, was controlled by the English Crown from the thirteenth century. Barriers to trade were made even more punitive by an Act of 1699, which stipulated that Irish fleece could only be exported through England and was additionally loaded with heavy tariffs, to avoid any clash with their own products. (This was the famous act that made it illegal to be buried in a shroud made of Irish wool, unless you were a victim of plague.) England had made its fortune on its fleeces (their Lord Chancellor still sits on a woolsack to reflect that), and didn't intend to allow its very profitable trade to be damaged.

And then there were the luxury goods for which the well-to-do of Ireland yearned. Brandy, tobacco, wine, tea, fine fabrics and laces were inordinately taxed on their way to this shore. What was more natural, then, than for gentlemen with a desire to promote local interests (and to improve their own incomes into the bargain) to gather like-minded helpers and circumvent these taxes by doing some shipping on their own? It took careful planning and strong courage to outwit the zealous English revenue cutters, but they did it. All round the coast, free trading was a way of life for centuries, and succeeded very well. Not only did the gentry profit: for many a poor family, the income derived from assisting in the smuggling game helped to keep them from starvation.

You needed a moonless night to avoid being seen. And of course you had to know your particular part of the coast very well, every inch of it and every hidden hazard, even in the pitch dark. The ideal location was one with several narrow

The free traders knew every inch, every inlet of their coastline.

secret inlets, the kind that might not be visible from the sea unless you knew exactly where they were. Then, reasonably easy access to a cave, a track, a farm building or friendly mansion, where the booty could be stored. But not for too long: it was vital to get the goods on their way to eager customers as quickly as possible, before searches were made by the preventative officers. Offshore islands were extremely helpful too, either as places to temporarily offload cargo or to conceal ships behind, out of sight of those unfriendly to their cause.

It went on all along our long and deeply indented sea coast for centuries. Generally, the east coast was the riskiest, as Britain was so close and Crown vessels patrolled the Irish Sea regularly. Nevertheless, places dangerously close to Dublin and Wexford saw their share of free trading also. Kinsale and

Cobh on the south coast were British garrison towns, but still knew a wily late-night trick or two. Often this was made easier by the discreet cooperation of local officials, who doubtless benefited by receiving an odd cask or bale.

The wilder coastlines fronting the Atlantic were the most suited to smuggling. Donegal was an ideal location for transatlantic ships to drop special barrels overboard by pre-arrangement; Sligo and Galway had remote headlands and bays, well away from the official ports where customs officers held sway; while West Cork and Kerry were exceptionally well placed for making swift and silent trips across to France and Flanders from a myriad of quiet coves.

The risks were high, and being caught could mean imprisonment or transportation. But the rewards were high too. Any man involved in the business at the top would have a known network of customers within his own area – eager clients

Deep inlets where a boat could lie concealed.

who would pay immediately for luxury goods and keep their mouths shut, as well as farmers and landowners who desperately wanted to get a reasonable return for their fleeces.

There would also be a network of local residents at the bottom of the social scale, those who warded off starvation by undertaking the hard work of loading boats late at night with heavy bales, or rowing out silently to a Dutch or French ship anchored well outside, getting their goods on board and taking back equally heavy loads of brandy, wine, tea, tobacco, velvets and laces.

Goods were transported up from the shore, often on backs bent low under the weight. Local horses and carts were borrowed for the night and returned before morning, with a small barrel or box tucked discreetly under a sack by way of payment. Grassy lanes lessened the noise, and many imposing houses of the gentry had a hidden cellar, concealed room or false chimney. The fellowship of free traders was a tight one, and its members knew better than to turn informer. To do so was to invite serious retribution from those with whom you had broken trust.

Some trading boats came as close to our shores as they dared; others made it their business to wait well outside the writ of the revenue officers, innocently pursuing their clearly visible craft of fishing, at the same time keeping a sharp eye out for small boats coming out from the mainland for a friendly visit. The *Freeman's Journal* in June 1764 quoted the complaints of one observer on the west coast who claimed that 'upwards of 100 sail of large French boats' were fishing for mackerel there, each with a 'string of nets that extends upwards of three miles'.

The local fishermen suffered, he said, but it was also sharply observed that this trespassing by their fishing rivals also concealed an active practice of transferring Irish wool to France, and bringing in tea, brandy and the like.

Galway was hugely involved in smuggling wool out to France and Flanders. Sheep were plentiful in that countryside, but to send fleeces legitimately through England meant getting virtually no return at all, due to the tariffs. Shipping it out illegally was hardly possible through Galway city's harbour, with revenue and customs officials always on the watch, but further out, there were many little harbours and inlets along the Connemara coast that were ideal for a smuggler's purpose. Carraroe, Roundstone, Clifden, with useful little islands and promontories behind which a boat could hide, saw a great deal of activity on moonless nights.

Even a ship leaving the city quays with a virtuously declared cargo could discreetly stop off on the coast to take on a more secret load. Returning from these profitable trips to mainland Europe, it was a simple matter to drop some barrels and packages off quietly at the same location, before continuing on openly to Galway city, where legitimate goods were declared and any necessary tariffs paid.

As a nice side-line to that wool export, it should be noted that the women of west-coast islands like Aran, Achill and Clare also spun the local fleece into yarn, which they then knitted into sturdy seaboot stockings. These were sold to visiting fishermen (and perhaps those supplying the smuggling trade) from France and Spain. A shilling a pair was the going rate in the mid-nineteenth century.

In the early nineteenth century, one John Black, a wealthy Sligo merchant and ship-owner, lived in some grandeur at Elsinore House, out on the coast by Rosses Point. By day a city gentleman, he transformed by night into one of the most successful smugglers of his day, known as Black Jack. Living out on the edge of Sligo Bay as he did, he could arrange for contraband goods to be discreetly dropped off by otherwise certified and legal ships (in all probability his own), which then continued on to the harbour quays with cargo to be openly declared to customs officials there. Later, he would send the untaxed goods onward to his many customers in the northwest. Through his energetic after-hours activities, he gave much-needed employment to local people, many of whom were living at or below the poverty line. They would grasp eagerly at the prospect of earning anything from loading, carrying, rowing and concealing, even though they would have been very aware that the danger was considerable.

Later in the nineteenth century, Elsinore House was bought by a cousin of the Yeats brothers, William and Jack, who spent most of their summer holidays there. Later, both attributed a great deal of their creative brilliance to the beauty of the area and its strong sense of history. Local tradition holds that a secret tunnel still runs from the cellars of Elsinore House to Deadman's Point, where ships once paused for contraband to be unloaded. And, naturally enough, the house is said to be haunted by the spirits of long-dead lawbreakers:

> *There were great cellars under the house, for it had been*
> *a smuggler's house a hundred years before, and sometimes*
> *three loud raps would come upon the drawing room*

window at sun-down, setting all the dogs barking, some dead smuggler giving his accustomed signal. One night I heard them very distinctly and my cousins often heard them, and later on my sister.

(*Reveries Over Childhood and Youth*, WB Yeats, 1916)

Smuggling was certainly a way of life on tiny Inishtrahull, just off Malin Head and the Inishowen Peninsula, the northernmost tip of Ireland. Islanders would watch for transatlantic cargo ships coming from the Americas, on their way to a big English port like Liverpool. Respectable merchants of Derry, down the long inlet of Lough Foyle, would have made arrangements well in advance.

Elsinore House then and now.

Barrels packed with contraband were tipped overboard as the ship moved slowly past. Once she had picked up speed again, continuing on towards her official destination, little local currachs would swiftly be launched to hook the floating barrels and bring them back to the island's shores. From the beach, these would be carried up and their contents concealed in secret passageways, under floors, even in the thatch of a roof, depending on the shape and size of the booty being hidden.

When the time was deemed safe, the goods would be shipped onwards by an innocuous-looking fishing boat, down the Lough to Derry, often late at night (but not too late for an equally innocent-looking donkey and cart to be standing by at a little-used quay, ready to unload the cargo and take it rattling over the cobbles to several destinations in the town).

The island of Inishtrahull did a roaring (free) trade.

The McCorkell family, merchants of Derry in the nineteenth century, did a lot of trading with the New World, taking out emigrants and bringing back principally rum, tobacco and cotton. For this they used their own sailing ship, the *Minnehaha*, built specially for them in Canada in 1860, with plenty of space below decks for either people or goods. (Local people affectionately called it the Green Yacht of Derry.) It undoubtedly dropped unofficial loads off Inishtrahull on its return voyages before delivering its legal cargo to those who had ordered it.

But other ships would have participated in this trade too. Crews on board many a nineteenth-century transatlantic vessel would have long-established contacts with those on land. It would have been well understood that anything dropped off in the sea by the offshore island would be spotted by eagle-eyed watchers and brought safely into hiding.

Did nothing go the other way? Of course it did. The Inishowen Peninsula is sparse, rocky and lacking in the generous fertility of other parts of Ireland, but if there is one thing it was ideal for, it was distilling good whiskey. Its inhabitants industriously saw to this, producing barrels upon barrels of it every year. A seriously remote location, a good damp climate for growing barley, plenty of turf to fire the still and, best of all, water on three sides. (It is always a good idea to have three exits if your business isn't quite in harmony with the law.)

The *poteen* or moonshine of Inishowen was renowned for its quality. It was much in demand, not only across Ireland, where it was discreetly sold at fairs and markets, but also to the east and to the west, in England and in the Americas. Smuggled barrels of 'the rale stuff' travelled far and wide, every shipment increasing the fame of Inishowen's hillside distillers. Of course, licensed businesses making legal liquor were furious, but catching a moonshiner in the act out on those wild, trackless hills was easier said than done, at a time when motor cars or indeed helicopters (let alone drones) had not been thought of.

One very clear, if unintended, effect of the smuggling industry, both on the island of Inishtrahull and on the Inishowen Peninsula, was that the standard of living among the communities there showed up in official reports as being surprisingly high. This puzzled the inspectors. The area, after all, was known to be one of the poorest in the country, so how could they be prospering?

As late as 1929, it was suggested in a government debate that free trading and spirited local entrepreneurship was still as active as ever in that part of Donegal. It had emerged that this was one of the very few places in the entire country where the population had actually increased by almost 100 percent. Could the local TD perhaps enlighten his respected colleagues? Well, he said innocently, they appeared to earn their livelihood from fishing. That was probably true anyway. If the fish they landed were rather bigger and heavier than a mackerel or a herring, then that was their business.

The collector of customs dues at Strangford Lough got more than he bargained for when he followed a report of smuggling in the autumn of 1784:

Whereas George Hamilton Esq, Collector of Strangford, having received Information that a considerable Quantity of Goods were intended to be

smuggled on the coast near Newcastle in the County
of Down did, with several Officers and Assistants, go
thither on the night of the 9th of September instant,
in order to intercept the same, in Case they should be
run; but on arriving at the Shore they found a very
great number of Men, with horses and carts, collected
on the Strand; and on advancing, many of the Men
swore that they would kill the said George Hamilton
Esq. and his assistants if they attempted to come near
them; and upon their proceeding, many Stones were
thrown at them, some of which struck the said George
Hamilton and one of his Assistants; and nearly at the
same Moment three Pistols or Guns were fired at them;
whereupon they returned the fire; and notwithstanding
that many more Stones were thrown, and the violent
Opposition given to them, they seized about a Ton
Weight of Tobacco, and some Horses and Cars.

This sort of thing would not do, said His Majesty's representatives, and both threats and inducements were accordingly
issued:

The Commissioners of His Majesty's Revenue, in
order to bring to speedy and condign Punishment the
Perpetrators of this most violent Outrage, hereby offer
a reward of Fifty Pounds for each of the three persons
concerned in throwing the said Stones, or firing upon
Mr Hamilton and his Assistants in the Execution of

their Duty as before mentioned, who shall, within six Months from the Date hereof, be first apprehended; to be paid on conviction.

And if any persons concerned therein except those who actually threw the Stone or Stones, or fired the said Shot or Shots at George Hamilton or his Assistants, will discover any of the accomplices in this Outrage, so that they, or any of them, shall be apprehended and convicted thereof, the Board will not only pay the Person or Persons making such discovery the Reward hereby offered, but will apply to Government for his or their Pardon. By Order of the Commmissioners. Thomas Winder, Dublin Castle, 29th September 1784.

Was more inducement needed? That was forthcoming too.

His Grace the Lord Lieutenant, for the better discovery and bringing to Justice the Persons concerned in committing the before mentioned Outrage on George Hamilton Esq, Collector of Strangford, and his Assistants, is pleased hereby to promise His Majesty's most gracious and free Pardon to any one of them (except those who actually threw the Stone or Stones, or fired the Shot or Shots at the said George Hamilton and his Assistants) who shall first discover his accomplices, so as they or any of them be apprehended and convicted of being guilty of the said outrage. By His Majesty's Command. Thomas Orde.

You would wonder if any of the men assembled on the beach that night were tempted enough by the extremely high reward offered, and informed on their associates. If they did, they would probably have had to leave the area with extreme speed, possibly even moving over to England if not further afield. Informers were, to put it mildly, not looked upon with favour or forgiveness. An official Crown pardon wouldn't have done them much good.

Skerries and Rush, north of Dublin, were known centres of smuggling in the eighteenth century. Despite the dangerous proximity of the capital, with its strong Crown presence, tea, tobacco, wines, spirits and even counterfeit money came in on boats known as 'cutters', designed to carry a great deal of cargo but still be fast enough to outrun the Excise officers. The smugglers of this region are said to have had their own secret language for communication, which no-one else could understand. It was known as *Fingallian*, after the old name for this region, *Fingal*, or Land of the Foreigners, named for the Viking community that settled here in earlier centuries.

One frequent destination for boats from Skerries and Rush was the Isle of Man, which acted as a handy *entrepôt* for international free traders. A frigate coming up from Spain could unload here and take back local goods, while the Irish cutter sailing over from Rush could provide those goods and stock up with Spanish wine, fine worked leathers and salt. A newspaper with the arresting title of *Pue's Occurrences* recorded in 1758:

> *At night George Weston Esq, Surveyor of Skerries, cruising off that coast in his barge, seized a large Smuggling Wherry with a great Quantity of Roll and Leaf Tobacco coming from the Isle of Man.*

Tax-free tobacco does seem to have been most in demand in the capital city, even over brandy, a fact which caused the authorities to thunder a warning in 1775:

> *Whereas great Quantities of Tobacco are smuggled into this Kingdom, assisted by the Assistance of Persons who harbour and conceal the same for the Proprietors; the Commissioners of His Majesty's Revenue think proper to give this publick Notice of the Law which enacts that: in case any Person shall knowingly harbour, keep or conceal, or shall knowingly suffer to be harboured, kept or concealed, or shall sell or expose to sale, or buy any exciseable Goods, knowing that the same were run, such Persons shall, over and above the Forfeiture of such Goods, forfeit treble the Value of such Goods. And the Board, on the memorial of the principal Merchants, Importers, and Manufacturers of Tobacco in this City, have resolved to prosecute all Persons who shall smuggle Tobacco, or harbour the same, and to levy without Remission all the Penalties which shall be inflicted according to Law.*
>
> (*Saunders' Newsletter*, 30 June 1775)

The *Hibernian Journal* of 26 June 1775 recorded the seizure off Dundrum by a Captain Adams, commander of the Townsend revenue cruiser, of:

> *A Large Smuggling Lugger with her entire Cargo, consisting of 61 Chests of Bohea Tea, 60 Anchors*

*of Brandy and Rum, and a large quantity of Roll
Tobacco, all which have been landed and lodged in His
Majesty's Store.*

The goods seized were valued at £2,500, showing just how
worthwhile the free trading business could be – so long as you
kept out of the clutches of the Revenue.

South of Dublin, the stretch of coastline between Bray
Head and Wicklow Head saw plenty of its own free trading
activities in the late eighteenth century. This was led by a man
called Murray, who dealt with Dutch frigates on a regular
basis. Further down in Wicklow, where visits from official-
dom were rare, free trading was rampant. A letter from Captain d'Auvergne, a British naval officer, to the authorities on
Jersey in 1799 warned:

*The communication of small smuggling vessels from
the latter part of the peninsula of Brittany is still
maintained with Ireland, and there is a French agent
at or near a place called Arklow, on the coast of Ireland,
who communicates with Roscoffm …*

West Cork, with that incredibly indented coastline, which
twists first one way and then the other, changing its mind and
its direction without warning, is packed with tiny harbours
and ancient grass-grown quays. There is often a rusted mooring ring still in place, and uneven, time-worn steps carved out
of the rocks themselves. Dutchman's Cove, tucked away in an
inaccessible location near Castletownshend, has old rock steps

The Brandy Hole, Crookhaven.

and even specially cut niches to hold dark lanterns. Streek Head above Crookhaven has several deep caves, including one still known as the Brandy Hole.

Canty's Cove, on the northern side of Mizen Head, had a reputation as a dangerous place for uninvited strangers. Canty, it is said, a practised free trader, would not hesitate to throw

Canty's Cove where many a secret cargo was run ashore.

such curious visitors from the back door of his clifftop house, straight down a sheer drop into the sea.

In such places, free traders reigned almost entirely undisturbed. Revenue officials would hesitate to make the hazardous trip from customs posts further along the coast, especially on dark nights, which is when the smugglers were most active.

There does seem to be some evidence that not only the local gentry, but often English settlers too (who would have been expected to set some kind of example in honouring Crown rules) were involved in these questionable activities. Sir William Hull, who owned that pilchard-salting industry at Crookhaven, seems to have been well mixed up in it. A Dutch sea captain, one Claes Campaine, regularly brought his frigate into Roaring Water Bay and moored close to Leamcon or Black Castle, the home of Sir William, so that the desirable tax-free goods could be ferried ashore in smaller boats. The purchasers, from the Lord Deputy to small merchants, were clearly notified in advance and were ready and waiting:

Thomas Neale of Bandonbridge, bought two bales of pepper, containing 700 weight, at 8d the lb., and 100 Barbary hides. Josua Boyle, of Waterford, bought one chest of camphor, 500 weight at least; 14 rolls of tobacco, 1000 weight of pepper, 212 lbs of cloves, 3 elephants' teeth, and 5 doz. red Muscovy hides. The two Whites, of Cork, carriers there, carried for most men and bought much themselves. Mr Jeremy Rostin, near Kinsale, bought tobacco and pepper. Mr Luxton, near Bandon-bridge, bought 300 weight of pepper. Mr Newcomen, of the Bridge, bought 800 weight of pepper. Sir Wm Hull sent 40 horse loads of pepper to Kinsale. Mr Nicholas Atwood confessed that the Deputy had from this pirate 6,000 weight of pepper and near 2,000 weight of wax. Mr Henry Turner of Bandonbridge bought much pepper and tobacco. Mr Alexander, dwelling near Castlelions, bought tobacco and other commodities to the value of £100 sterling. Sir Lawrence Parsons' men traded there; and John Forde bought 24 bundles of red hides, wherein was divers parcels of fine Hollands …

(*Irish Calendar of State Papers, 1615–25*)

If officials set to guard the Crown's interests in some parts of the country were immune to temptation or bribery, other methods could be brought into play to avoid discovery. SC Hall, who penned his *Retrospect of a Long Life* in 1883, recalled a memorable visit of his young days:

> In 1818 I was a visitor at a house in the vicinity of Castletownsend, Co. Cork. My host was a gentleman high in position and of ancient descent, and my summer holiday was spent at his large and proverbially hospitable mansion on the sea coast. He was then about the most extensive smuggler in Ireland, and had reconciled his conscience to his calling on the ground that he had been heavily fined for some comparatively venial offence against the revenue laws. I had frequently expressed to his sons a desire to see something of the proceedings of a regular smuggling raid, and especially to visit one of the smuggling ships.

The opportunity soon offered itself. Knowing that the correct combination of weather and moon phase was nigh, his genial host threw a grand ball, to which of course he invited the officers of the neighbouring garrison as well as the Commissioner of Excise. The party (intentionally) went on till late, and beds were civilly offered to all the half-tipsy guests, who were glad to avail of them. Young Hall, however, had been given a clear hint to be wide awake and ready …

An hour or so after midnight I found myself hurrying down from the house to the shore. The beach was crowded with vehicles of every description, the common car being by far the most numerous. These cars were rapidly filling and passing off. In a picturesque cave sat my host, a rude table covered with banknotes before him. He was receiving money and giving orders for the delivery of tobacco, gin, brandy, tea, and other commodities which were unloaded from the boats as they put into the shore from a vessel anchored a few cables' length off.

Hall insisted on going back in one of the boats to see the Dutch frigate that lay outside, and was civilly offered a glass of schnapps in the captain's cabin. While he was enjoying this, an alarm was sounded, as a strange boat had been sighted rounding the point:

It was well known that a revenue cutter lay moored on the other side of an intervening promontory; the hatches were at once battened down and preparations made for resistance. As there was no boat alongside, I should have been in the position of the daw with stolen feathers; but fortunately the intruder was merely a fishing hooker. He was made to heave to; compensation was given for the delay by sending an anker of spirits on board, and I was not sorry to find myself in the last boat making for the shore.

Getting back to bed in the early dawn, Hall realised that the officers and the Commissioner had slept peacefully throughout the night. Perhaps their door had been stealthily locked; perhaps it hadn't. The beach and cave, in the meantime, were rendered as smooth and empty as if nothing had happened. Later on that day, it emerged that the coastguard had indeed been alerted to the possible presence of a smuggling ship, but had required the orders of the Commissioner of Excise to do anything about it. Since that official was not to hand, the matter rested there. Good planning, certainly, on the part of the Gentleman of Castletownsend.

There were similar set-ups in the small inlets of Kerry, especially around spacious Tralee Bay. Once Tralee town, with its newly built canal, became the major port, smaller harbours in outer reaches of the bay, were neglected. Once busy with com-

Barrow near Fenit, Co. Kerry, a well-known landing place for smugglers.

mercial traffic, they were now mostly forgotten by the revenue men. Not by the smugglers, though.

The small tidal creek of Barrow, near Fenit, saw its off-the-record trading grow exponentially once Crown attention had shifted to Tralee. Many of the large houses of the gentry in the vicinity had hidden cellars, false walls, even an extra chimney or two, where recently landed goods could be swiftly tucked away. In 1784, the *Freeman's Journal* reported that the merchants and tobacco manufacturers of Limerick had presented a petition to parliament, complaining of 'the great loss and damages they suffer from the vast quantities of tobacco landed and smuggled into the county of Kerry and its neighbouring districts'.

The free traders didn't always get away with it though. Earlier, in 1775, the *Hibernian Journal* carried an account of a successful capture:

> *Seized on the 23rd ult on the coast of Kerry, by Captain Richard Bowden, Captain of His Majesty's Revenue Cruiser, The Dungannon, and John Spring Esq, Surveyor of Dingle, the cargo of a Smuggling Vessel which was landed, consisting of sixty-one tierces and sixteen ankers of French Brandy, and sixteen packs of Tobacco, which are lodged in His Majesty's Stores of Tralee.*

The most fascinating stories of Kerry smuggling, however, come from the home of one of our most famous historical figures, Daniel O'Connell. O'Connell, as an MP at Westminster, achieved Catholic emancipation for his people, and fought for

Derrynane House, home of Daniel O'Connell, saw a great deal of free trading throughout its existence.

a separate Irish parliament all his life. Known as The Liberator, he belonged to a wealthy and powerful family, which had its seat at Derrynane by Caherdaniel.

The family home still stands, tall and secretive, above its own private bay, and here some of the most daring and courageous exploits of the free trading age took place. Derrynane Bay is one of those hidden inlets that is not visible from the sea, and needs excellent local knowledge to be found at all.

'Farming, sporting, and smuggling attracted several old Catholic families to these wild and remote shores, where they could worship unmolested, and earn something to boot,' explains Morgan O'Connell in *The Last Colonel of the Irish Brigade*, published in 1892. 'Their faith, their education, their wine, and their clothing were equally contraband.'

Much of that may have happened before The Liberator himself was born in 1775, but it is entirely likely that the young

Daniel did occasionally lend a hand in unloading cargo from boats beached on the shore, rolling barrels of brandy or wine up to the handy dry cave nearby, and perhaps taking rolls of sumptuous fabric up to the house for the women to seize and gloat over. Tea was much prized, as were sugar and tobacco, rum and brandy. Small quantities of claret were also imported, for the O'Connells' sole use, according to their descendant. (Remember that most of these well-born Irish landowners, being denied an education in the land of their birth because of their religion, had received it in France. This goes a long way to explain their renowned polish and *savoir faire* under all conditions.)

Butter, salt, hides and salt fish were the main items exported; wool was sent too, but interestingly this and linen seem to have been the perquisite of the ladies of Derrynane. It gives rise to a pleasant image of these gentlewomen sitting and singing at their spinning, or welcoming local farmers to the

Derrynane Bay, where many boats slipped in and out on dark nights.

back door with bales of fleece, while making arrangements with the men of the house to ship these goods out on the next available boat. How eagerly they must have awaited the boat's return, perhaps with some exquisite velvet or lace for their new gowns. In later centuries, countrywomen relied on the 'egg money' from the poultry they tended to keep them going. The womenfolk of Caherdaniel had an eye to the main chance a great deal earlier.

More than butter and wool were smuggled out, though. There was a human element too. Young men desirous of fighting for Ireland's freedom were spirited across to France in this manner, to join the Irish Brigade there. It was forbidden by the English Crown of course, and those discovered escaping could be hanged; but many seized the chance to make the crossing, concealed below deck on a laden frigate, to join an elite corps of the French army, where the commands were traditionally given in Irish. Daniel Charles O'Connell, uncle of the Liberator, was the last colonel of the Brigade, rising to the rank of General.

An eighteenth-century letter survives from O'Connell family records that is worth quoting in full, as it gives such a vivid picture of the complex organisation behind the smuggling carried on from Derrynane alone. It is written by Maurice, very obviously a sharp man of business:

> *Darrinane, 7ber 22ⁿᵈ, 1754.*
> *Dr Sir, I have wrote to you ys afternoon, The Alexander, Captain John Fitzgerald, on brd, which have shipped, for account of Messrs Seggerson and company, 2 large Sacks wool, one of which is for the*

Captain and Crew; 58 firkins butter, and 65 salt Hydes … She set out with a Very favourable Wind and the strongest appearance of the continuance of it … The whole Proceeds are to be invested for Teas, half Green and half Bohea. As to last commodity, it promises pretty well. Brandy is in noe demand, nor is there likelihood for a Call for it for a considerable time.

I mentioned to you in said letter to send 13 Ankers brandy, 3 of which Cherry. A cask powder Sugar, and 2 Tierces good Claret for ye private consumption, and separate account of Messrs Seggerson and my ffather which please to observe, and am ord'red to direct you to send two Quarter-casks small White St Martin or Rhenish wine for ye same purpose and account. The costs and charges of all which charge to a separate account.

You have in charge £10 or £17 for Butter, ye property of my ffather. He thinks proper, in consequence of ye stuff, to order home the proceeds of the Butter in Teas as before.

This you are to note, and, as it is made over on me, The Goods are to be marked over with the Initial letters of my Name. There are ffourteen Hydes of my own, and 160 bandles flannell of my Mother's, in 2 bundles. Out of which pay Cornilius 60 livres, and send the 4 Aunes Velvet mention'd. The price of the Looking … [probably looking glass, of which two still survive at Derrynane] *deduct from the price of ye last-mentioned Butter.*

> *Advise us speedily of yr Vessel's arrival and course*
> *of the Markett, and dispatch her with all possible*
> *Expedition. We'll endeavour to send her Back*
> *immediately after her arrival. Mr Tim McCarthy*
> *prays you will ensure £30 stg on 35 hydes, 3 firkins*
> *butter, and a pack of wool he has on board. Your*
> *brother Jemmy has shipped himself according to your*
> *Directions. I fancy my brother Connell has ere now*
> *advised you of his arrival in Caen.*
>
> *I am, dear Cousin,*
> *your sincere Kinsman and obedient Servant,*
> *Maurice Connell.*
>
> (quoted in *The Last Colonel of the Irish Brigade*, op. cit.)

One notices the mention of two other members of the family – Jemmy and Maurice's own brother, who have already crossed to France. Were they heading for the French army and the Irish Brigade, or getting some experience in the Continental end of the O'Connell family business?

The Messrs Seggerson mentioned in the second line of the letter were Cork city merchants, based at Dunscombe's Marsh, with a good river frontage for landing. Clearly, Maurice O'Connell's network of contacts stretched far and wide. The goods destined for the Seggerson emporium would go up from Derrynane by boat, doubtless well hidden under more legal cargo.

Perhaps one of the most surprising smuggled exports was salt to England. In order to raise money for his military campaigns,

William III decided to tax domestic salt, an essential provision for every household and many industries. Oddly enough, this unwelcome tax did not apply in Ireland, and this naturally led to a positive explosion of smuggling across the Irish Sea. The ancient salt industry that had survived so far on the east coast of England (Salthouse Heath in Norfolk still bears the name) went under as a result.

Of course, improved controls and better organisation by customs and revenue officers as the nineteenth century went on inevitably caused some reduction in smuggling, but it was England's move towards a policy of actual free trade from the 1840s onward that saw its real decline. The great days (nights, rather) of choosing your time, watching the clouds, keeping a look-out, hastily unloading and loading, upping anchors and heading off hastily were drawing to a close. The gentlemen in country houses around the coast heaved a sigh for the nights of glory gone, and sent the footman down to count the bottles still remaining in the cellar.

Mute testament to those gone far away, never to return.

CHAPTER VII

Travelling Far From Home

T he *imramma*, or legendary travel tales, opened this book, but there were many genuine journeys far across the sea. Throughout the centuries, many people left this island to sail across the oceans, whether in religious zeal, through necessity, or in search of adventure. Some came back; many did not. They deserve to be remembered.

Medieval Irish monks saw it as their duty to spread the word abroad in darkest Europe, and did so whenever they got the chance, setting up monasteries in France, Switzerland, Italy and even further afield. They would have headed for the nearest busy port, taken passage on one of the many boats loading up for foreign trade, and set out on foot when that first destination was reached, sublimely sure of their mission and its success.

The Abbey of St Gall in Switzerland is one such, said to have been founded by one of the twelve monks who accompanied St Columbanus on his proselytising mission to the Continent. It has one of the oldest monastic libraries in the world. Bobbio, in Italy, another Columbanus foundation, possessed one of the greatest libraries of medieval times. Marmoutier in Alsace, Luxeuil in Burgundy and more, all flourished due to the zeal of the Irish monks. Today, the many ancient Irish texts held in the seclusion of European religious foundations are testament to the wanderings of those early monks. If you can't find an old Irish document here at home, you might well have success in central Europe.

Where the monks led, pilgrims followed. The road to Santiago de Compostela, the shrine of St James on the north coast of Spain, is still traversed today by those searching for something beyond the ordinary. To walk it is to see still in place the ancient, tiny bridges, the crumbling hostelries and the sign of the scallop shell that told weary travellers over the centuries that they could find rest close by. To start on such a journey meant putting your affairs in order, since the way was dangerous and you might not return. If you did survive the ordeal and came safely home, you treasured a silver scallop shell among your proudest possessions, as proof that you had walked the pilgrim path.

Travellers from France traditionally set out from a particular inn in Paris and made their way south to cross the Pyrenees at the Breche de Roland. They then descended into Galicia and the dry dusty roads of northern Spain. English pilgrims might go from small ports like St John's in Cornwall, where blessings on their journey were given at a tiny church. Irish travellers would have to find trading vessels sailing from Waterford or Cork to Bordeaux or, if they were fortunate, northern Spain itself, which would cut out much of the foot slogging over the high mountains. Whatever the route taken, it was an enormously challenging one, but would certainly have widened many a pilgrim's horizons.

Simon's journey to the Holy Land

One very determined medieval monk from Clonmel conceived the idea of travelling all the way to the Holy Land. Symon Semeonis (or Simon FitzSimon) was probably of Norman origin, and well-educated, since he was able to work out the complex route across Europe (perhaps an ancestor had gone on the Crusades?) and presumably was also able to source the finances demanded by such a huge journey.

He managed to obtain the permission and blessing of his abbot at the Franciscan Friary of Clonmel. Then, taking thought that a companion would be a good idea on such a long journey, he went round to the chilly scriptorium, where diligent scribes worked on wonderfully decorative religious texts, and persuaded a fellow monk to put down the quill and ink and come with him.

What is more, he wrote up his experiences in a detailed diary when he got back. The world should be truly grateful for *Itinerarium fratrum Symonis Semeonis et Hugonis illuminatoris* (The Itinerary of Brother Symon Semeonis and Hugh the Illuminator). It captures scenes, people and cultures of the time in such a vivid way that you actually see them as he did so long ago.

In 1323, then, FitzSimon (we should really call him Simon the Backpacker, since he heralded, by many centuries, the hippy trails of later generations) sets off from Clonmel with Hugh. Tramping to the east coast, they find a boat to take them to Wales, and then continue down through Canterbury to Dover, and across to Wissant, near modern Calais. Paris is visited, and boats taken downriver to Marseilles. A sea crossing to Genoa, then a hot, dusty journey down through Verona and Padua to wealthy Venice, which Simon admires greatly.

On they go, through Albania (Simon providing in his diary one of the first detailed accounts of that country) and into the Aegean Sea, voyaging past several Greek islands. They land on Crete, where they are very much impressed with the excellent wine and fresh fruits to be had.

Crossing to Alexandria, they are delayed by officials who search their baggage, discovering holy medals, which they considered heathen. The security guards correspond with the Sultan at Cairo by carrier pigeon, enquiring what should be done with these suspicious travellers. While waiting for the return pigeon flight and the hoped-for permission to proceed, Simon and Hugh explore the city, Simon describing clothing, jewellery, social customs and foodstuffs, even the coinage used, and the cost of different items.

Eventually permitted to continue, they take a canal boat down to Old Babylon, delighted to spot crocodiles along the way, and on to Cairo, which was at that time a vast and very rich city. Here they admire elephants and giraffes, and see the precious balsam trees, heavily protected by guards because of their value. They visit the Pyramids, and hear tales of a secret tunnel that leads from these, underneath the Nile, and emerges at a temple some distance away. It is entirely possible – several such tunnels have been identified under pyramids elsewhere – but the tale could also have been part of the already polished tourist industry of the time.

In Cairo, alas, Hugh the Illuminator is taken ill of a local fever and dies, leaving Simon to travel on alone to the Holy Land, grieving for the loss of his friend. He does take the precaution of getting a travel permit from the Sultan, which will allow him to visit the most holy places without being stopped or made to pay taxes. This important passport is authorised by the Sultan's own drawing of his hand, without which it would be valueless. As he journeys, FitzSimon gives marvellous descriptions of the endless desert, the nomads with their tents, and the walled enclosures that have been set up by the Sultan a day's march apart, so travellers always have somewhere to shelter at nightfall.

At last, our backpacking pilgrim fulfils his heart's desire and reaches Jerusalem and the Sepulchre of Our Lord. The account stops here, but presumably Simon returns home by much the same route, since he lives to write down the details of everything he has seen on his incredible journey. It surely must have been the most eagerly sought and greedily perused document in the abbey library thereafter, one imagines, since it conjures up such wonderful images of far-off lands and wonders hitherto unknown.

The origins of the Claddagh ring?

Some who set off from Ireland with one future in mind found themselves instead in very different circumstances. In 1675, the young Richard Joyce of Galway, then aged fifteen, wanted to seek his fortune. He signed up with a local agent to work as an indentured servant in the West Indies (this was a handy way for impoverished younger sons to pay the cost of passage through their subsequent labour), and duly embarked with excited anticipation.

Unfortunately, the ship was seized by those ever-active corsairs of the Barbary Coast, and Richard, along with the rest of the passengers and crew, was sold into slavery in Algiers. He ended up as assistant to a well-established goldsmith there, and made the best of this change in his plans, working early and late and developing considerable skill in designing jewellery. As an indentured servant, he would have had to work pretty hard in the West Indies anyway, so perhaps it wasn't such a bad alternative. As subsequent events show, he certainly seems to have won his master's confidence and impressed that man with his reliability and skill.

In 1689, under the orders of William III that all his subjects held captive in North Africa should be set free, Richard Joyce, now twenty-nine, was released. His master was dismayed. Realising he might be losing a valued assistant,

A Claddagh ring sign in Galway.

he offered the young man half of his business and even his daughter in marriage if he would stay. Joyce, however, wanted to return home to Galway and his family, and that is what he did. Setting up in business as a jeweller, he is credited with designing the first Claddagh ring, quite possibly from a design he saw in Algiers.

Who, seeing that graceful shape of hands clasped around a heart – traditionally the gift of a lover – in a Galway shop window, would connect it to the hot, dusty streets of Algiers, the shouts of vendors, the scent of exotic spices, the bleats of sheep and goats, the gleam of strange fruits; and a dark workroom, the workman bent over his bench, dreaming of home?

Emigration

Emigrants have been part of Ireland's history since long before the Famine of the mid-nineteenth century saw the endless trickle grow to a massive flood. Searching for work, for a better life, to give their children a future, and of course escaping starvation, many found their way to America, Canada, Australia and other New World lands, settling down and founding their own dynasties, but never forgetting their Irish roots.

The many yearning songs and ballads that date from those days demonstrate the longing for home that must have imbued every waking moment for so many emigrants. Some deal with the pain of parting from family and a dearly-loved place:

> *So farewell to my mother, my father adieu,*
> *My sister and my brother, farewell unto you,*
> *I am bound for America, my fortune to try,*
> *When I think on Bunclody, I'm ready for to die …*
> *Others remember nostalgically the peace and gentle life*
> *of the Irish countryside, so very different to the huge*
> *bustling cities in which they now found themselves:*
> *Oh that little rugged boreen far away,*
> *Where the people sat at evening in the shadow of the*
> *trees,*
> *And with voices low and gentle as the whispering of*
> *the breeze,*
> *Passed the time in song and story*
> *Till the stars came out in glory,*
> *O'er that little rugged boreen far away.*

Very few accounts survive written by the poorer emigrants. Diaries and memoirs are the province of the well-educated and usually the financially secure. The poor had enough to do keeping body and soul together, saving their energy for the struggle to survive. There is, however, a heartrending description of departure from the Great Blasket Island in Maurice O'Sullivan's *Twenty Years A-Growing*.

Maurice's sister Maura is determined to head for Springfield in Massachusetts, where many relatives have already found work in the factories. At first, she and her friend Kate are excited at the prospect, promising each other that they will explore all the big, fine shops the very day they get there. But when her passage money arrives, she starts to realise what she is leaving behind.

> *Maura was crying every day now. 'Musha, I don't know in the world,' she would say when she washed the plates, 'will the day ever come when I will be washing these again?' It was the same when she would be sweeping the floor. She would look at the broom and the tears would fall. Then she would run across to my dog, Rose, and catch her up in her arms. 'Musha, Roseen, isn't it many a day the two of us were west on the White Strand, I throwing stones into the water and you swimming out after them!' and Rose would wag her tail and bark for joy for Maura to be playing with her.*

The 'wake' held on the evening before departure was even more distressing among island communities than on the mainland,

So many young people left
the Blasket Islands to find
a better life.

if that were possible, since the entire population would have lived closely together and been more like one family than several. The tearing apart of that community was hard for those who were left behind, harder still for those who faced an entirely new life from the moment they landed, with little time in it indeed to stroll around the fine shops so eagerly anticipated by Maura and Kate.

Although personal memoirs are few, what have survived are the records of an incredible number of letters sent home to Ireland from America by young women, enclosing money orders or prepaid tickets for their relatives. Working principally in domestic service (and thus not having to expend wages on rent), they saved every penny possible to enable a sadly missed brother or sister to come out and join them, lessening the loneliness, creating a new home from home. The Irish-American publisher Matthew Carey estimated that for the years 1835 and 1836 alone, the total of monies sent to Ireland exceeded $800,000, most of it in very small drafts, often under $25. So much thought, so much scrimping and watching every coin, went into every one of

How many hopeful letters to America did this old Victorian postbox receive?

those money orders, carefully obtained from one of the emigrant savings banks (of which there were many in the poorer districts of New York, to take just one example). They would be addressed with loving care to the old family home, and sent off from the post office with a surge of delighted hope that soon a familiar face would be joining the sender. Records of the American postal service have shown that between 1854 and 1875, more than 30 million such letters were sent back to Ireland.

Those who could not rely on family already in America to send the passage money might nevertheless find themselves on an emigrant ship as part of an assisted scheme by one of the big (usually English) landowners in Ireland. Lord Lansdowne, for example, who owned 95,000 acres in Kerry, much of it in the rough and stony land around Kenmare, sent over 1,700 of his poorest tenants to New York in 1851. His agent selected each week from the overcrowded workhouse 200 of those he judged most suited to emigration, and put them in the charge of an employee for the sixty-mile journey to Cork. It is all too likely that they had to walk the entire way, which in their already exhausted and enfeebled situation would not have been easy.

Lord Palmerston (afterwards to become British prime minister) was helping tenants to emigrate from his Sligo lands even before the inexorable calamity of the Famine made it a necessity. When that disaster did strike, he increased his efforts. In 1847, no fewer than nine chartered ships left Sligo, carrying about 2,000 Palmerston-assisted emigrants, destined for British North America. Unfortunately, one at least did not make it safely across the Atlantic: the *Carrick,* which sailed at the end of April in that year, was, in late May, driven by gales on to dangerous shoals off Cape Rosarie. She went to pieces, with no more than twenty-two of the 200 passengers saved, although all the crew survived.

There seems to be some evidence that Palmerston instructed his agents to make some provision for clothing and food for these emigrants, unlike Lord Lansdowne, whose former tenants were forced to survive the voyage with little or nothing. Nevertheless, those who did survive the appalling onboard conditions arrived determined to make something of this new chance, to carve out a better life for themselves and their children. Living conditions might have been rough by American standards, but for those who had known nothing but the mud floor of a stone cabin, it might well have seemed desirable.

As time went on, and the number of Irish immigrants grew in large cities, those yet to come could rely on a strong and welcoming network to help them fit in. There were friends and relatives who knew the old ways and would ease them into the new. And above all, there was work to be had, opportunities to be chased. There are several instances of Irish women setting up boarding houses in the tougher districts, like Five Points in New York for example, and building up satisfying bank balances.

You only have to look at the immensely strong Irish network in America today to see how their children continued with that same determination, moving ever forward and upward. When, a century or more later, descendants of those first emigrants came across the Atlantic to visit the land of

The old cottage still waits for those emigrants to return.

their forefathers, they must have experienced strong emotions as they looked on the ruined cottages, the grassy laneways and the coastal paths of which they had heard so much from their grandparents and great-grandparents.

There are so many of these ruined cottages and deserted hamlets all around Ireland, and on the offshore islands too –mute evidence of emigration, the breaking-up of families, the end of generations living in one place, making a living, tending their crops and livestock. To stand in front of one of these crumbling stone houses is to sense the heartbreak and agony that echoed around its worn doorstep and its familiar walls as, one after another, its inhabitants packed their bundles and left, stepping down the pathway, opening the old wooden gate for the last time, turning to say goodbye to the place where they had been born, had grown up listening to the sound of the stream, the wind in the trees, the calls of the cattle in the little field beyond. Before them an unknown future, behind everything they held dear. Perhaps they vowed to return one day.

When the Irish diaspora was at its peak, crowded ships would leave from the two major emigration points, Cork in the south and Moville on Lough Foyle in the north, carrying huge numbers to a new life. An elderly lady living at the edge of Cork harbour remembers an even older lady telling her as a child that all along both sides of Cork harbour, the friends and relatives of those leaving would light little bonfires in farewell and stand beside them, waving, until the sea took the vessel out of sight. Exactly the same custom prevailed for many years at Moville, as the boat steamed out past

Inishowen Head and turned west into the wide Atlantic. How the emigrants must have gazed back, keeping those fires in sight as long as possible, and taking their last farewell of the familiar green fields of home.

There is one strange instance of assisted emigration from an earlier era that deserves attention. This is the conveying of Irish tenantry to the coast of Newfoundland by their English landlord, George Calvert (Lord Baltimore), in the seventeenth century. (Despite its name, the manor of Baltimore to which the title appertains is in the Irish midlands, and has nothing to do with the West Cork harbour where the attack by Barbary pirates took place.)

Lord Baltimore was one of those who saw a bright future in establishing settlements overseas. Having purchased a large

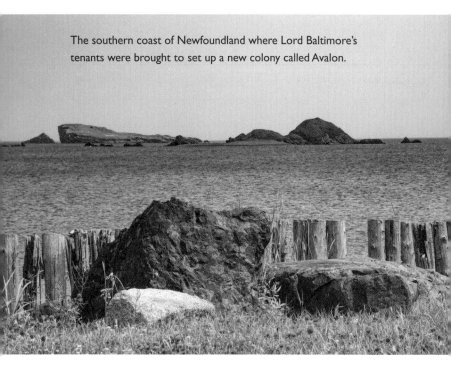

The southern coast of Newfoundland where Lord Baltimore's tenants were brought to set up a new colony called Avalon.

area of land in the south of Newfoundland, he saw a good opportunity for his impoverished tenants and made arrangements to bring them over. He romantically christened the new settlement Avalon, where the first shipload of immigrants arrived from the Longford region in 1621.

Although the southern coastline of Newfoundland was probably already well known to seasonal fishermen, it would have been a strange new world to these immigrants, with a much harsher climate than they had been accustomed to. Lord Baltimore himself, after enduring several winters here with his family ('... so intolerable cold as it is hardly to be endured ...'), decided that his future lay down in milder climes on Chesapeake Bay, and left his new settlement to fend for itself while he worked on developing the community in Maryland that would bear his name forever after as the port of Baltimore.

In the meantime, the people of Avalon survived somehow, augmented each year by the visits of the fishermen, many of whom might have stayed on when they found a real settlement there to join. As is so often the case, although the lords and their ladies who first set up Avalon are well documented, no record has yet been found of the names of those first immigrants, who formed a strong foundation for Newfoundland's future. Currently, detailed excavation work at Avalon is ongoing, revealing much of the infrastructure of their lives in this new land.

Seasonal fishermen of course spread all along the coasts of Newfoundland and Nova Scotia, often staying on after the season had ended, marrying locally and setting up as farmers.

Stories from the Sea

The proliferation of Irish names on signposts, hoardings, shop fronts and newspaper advertisements makes it clear just how many Irish lads who joined the English boats heading north for the fishing actually decided to stay on, marry locally, and work the land that at least offered some freedom and space. The names in graveyards too are testimony to those who came.

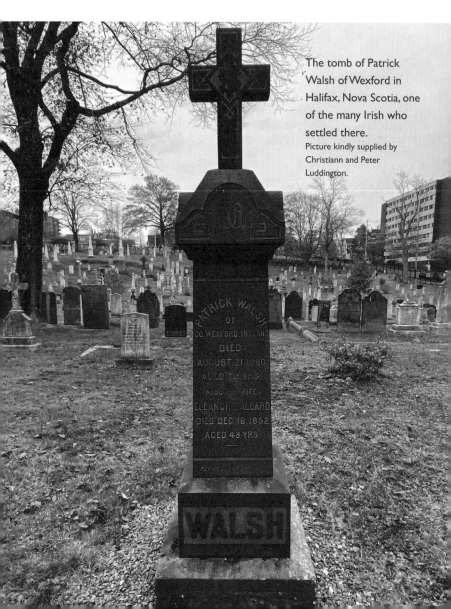

The tomb of Patrick Walsh of Wexford in Halifax, Nova Scotia, one of the many Irish who settled there.
Picture kindly supplied by Christiann and Peter Luddington.

Tom Crean

Finally, a more recent tale of one who travelled far and came safely home again. A young Kerryman, who joined the Royal Navy while still underage, went on to make history as a brave explorer and determined survivor under unimaginably harsh conditions.

Tom Crean was born in 1877 on the family farm near Annascaul, one of ten children. Here, life was hard enough to toughen a young man, but the opportunities to prosper and get ahead were virtually nil. The choices were stark enough: emigration or joining the English forces. Hardly surprising then that he joined the Navy in 1892, pretending he was a year older than he actually was. Crean got on well in his chosen career, showing himself adaptable and energetic. In 1901, while serving on a ship in New Zealand, he heard of Robert Scott's proposed expedition to Antarctica. He lost no time in offering his services for this great adventure.

Although they were both in the Navy, Scott having joined at the age of thirteen and Crean at fifteen, their worlds couldn't have been further apart. The service at that time had rigorous divisions between officers and other ranks, but even the privileged upper echelons realised that they couldn't hope to mount a successful expedition without hardworking men of the lower orders. Crean had already proved his worth as a reliable seaman, and so was one of those chosen for the momentous project.

That first Antarctic voyage, the *Discovery* Expedition of 1901–04, had the official aim of carrying out scientific research and geographical exploration in this, the last

Statue of Tom Crean in his native Annascaul.

unexplored continent. Really though, the overriding aim was to 'bag' the South Pole for Britain before any other country got there.

The expedition didn't succeed, although they got further south than anyone had done before, and in the effort survived appalling conditions and near-starvation. The *Discovery*, in fact, remained trapped in solid ice for two years, sometimes with temperatures falling below -54 degrees Celsius, before finally breaking free and allowing the expedition to return to northern waters.

The venture had, however, given Crean a chance to demonstrate his ability to survive (even two near-fatal falls through the ice into the waters below didn't dampen his ardour). He had shown himself to be calm and practical, capable of carrying out orders and also of displaying extreme bravery. This Robert Scott recognised, formally recording Tom as having given 'meritorious service throughout', and recommending him for promotion. Crean was also extremely popular among the expedition members generally, his Irish wit and habit of breaking into song at the most stressful moments proving useful in the often desperate circumstances.

Ernest Shackleton (another Irishman, born in Kildare but brought up in England), had also been on that *Discovery* voyage. He decided to try his own luck in 1907 with the *Nimrod* expedition, but this again failed. On hearing this, Scott is said to have remarked to Crean, who was serving on his ship, 'I think we had better have a shot next.'

Of course, the Kerryman, who had proved his worth on the earlier voyage, was included on the team for the *Terra Nova*

Expedition of 1911–13. They set out in June 1910, and reached Melbourne, Australia, in October of that year. Here, Scott received a numbing shock, in the form of a telegram from the Norwegian explorer Roald Amundsen, on board his ship *Fram*:

> *Beg to inform you Fram proceeding Antarctic –*
> *Amundsen.*

Now the gloves were off, so to speak, and Scott could waste no time. Tom Crean, too, desperately wanted to be the first Irishman to stand at the South Pole. But the odds were already heavily stacked against them. Amundsen had been brought up with cold and snow, and knew the techniques of tackling these efficiently. He knew the right clothing to wear and how to handle dog sleds, and was an expert on skis. Scott, on the other hand, preferred to trust good old British clothing (totally inadequate in Antarctic conditions) and was much opposed to dog sleds, preferring the exhausting and inefficient method of dragging heavily laden sleds by manpower. Possibly that was because he didn't want to copy Amundsen – we shall never know.

While on the *Terra Nova* expedition, Crean undertook two of his most courageous feats, either of which could easily have claimed his life. The first was when he and two other members of the team found themselves stranded on a small floe in breaking ice with some of their sled ponies, surrounded by eager killer whales. By leaping from one rocking floe to another, and eventually clambering his way up onto a solid ice cliff, Crean managed to make his way back to base camp and bring help to rescue his comrades. The ponies, alas, did not survive.

In November 1911, Tom Crean was in the group of eight that got to within 270km (168 miles) of the Pole. Now Scott made a strange decision, excluding Crean from the final small party and sending him back to base camp instead, with two others. It is said that Crean wept when he realised he was not to be allowed to proceed. Why Scott didn't include him is hard to comprehend. Crean was, after all, one of the strongest, most capable and most experienced members of the party, and totally reliable. Perhaps it had something to do with Scott's old-world views on rank and status, and the rights of a particular class to achieve such an important goal. Again, we shall never know. One does wonder, however, if things might have turned out differently had the leader allowed this loyal man to take part in the last lap.

The whole world knows what happened to Scott and his party. They managed to get to the Pole, suffering incredible privation, only to find that Amundsen had beaten them to the prize. They started back, exhausted and wretched, but never made it.

What are less well-known are the experiences of Crean and his two companions, Lashly and Evans, who had to struggle back to base camp, a journey of incredible difficulty. At one point, in desperation, they actually slid 2,000 feet down a glacier, avoiding bottomless crevasses by sheer luck. Now Evans became seriously ill (probably scurvy among other things, since their diet was hardly enough to hold body and soul together) and it became evident that he could not go on.

This was another moment for Crean to show his mettle. Lashly would stay and care for Evans, while he went on ahead and tried to reach Hut Point, where help might be got. Leaving virtually all the remaining rations with his comrades, he set out with just two sticks of chocolate and three biscuits to walk the 56km (35 miles) across wild and inhospitable icy terrain. He made it in eighteen hours, in a state of total collapse, and was able to organise a rescue party.

'Well, sir, I was very weak when I reached the hut ...'

It was for this feat of endurance, in saving the life of Evans, that Crean and Lashly were afterwards awarded the Albert Medal.

It was by now grimly accepted that the final group heading for the Pole had not survived. Almost a year later, Crean was one of the party that went in search of Scott and his companions, eventually discovering the sad truth in a half-hidden tent amid the snow, some short distance from the Pole. Finding the bodies, and reading Scott's final letter, they learned how it had ended.

By his next action, Crean showed himself to be truly one of nature's great gentlemen. Among the search party was a Norwegian member of the expedition named Tryggve Gran. Emerging from the tent, heartbroken at the finding of Scott's body, Crean walked steadily up to Gran. He told him the news, and then shook him by the hand, congratulating him on Norway having first reached the South Pole. How many others would have thought of doing that? Gran never forgot the delicate courtesy of that action. And it tells us a great deal about the man that was Tom Crean.

You honestly might have thought that such experiences were more than enough for any one man. By this time, Tom Crean was thinking about his later years, and had just bought a run-down pub in his home village of Annascaul, with the intention of making that his future. However, when Ernest Shackleton decided on yet another adventure in 1914, he asked Crean to join the team, and the Kerryman just couldn't resist the call of the wild south.

The Imperial Trans-Antarctic Expedition was to attempt to cross the entire icy continent from one side to the other, with a crew from another ship at the opposite end, placing food stores at intervals along the route. In the process, they would learn much about the geography and wildlife of the region.

The expedition in fact set sail just as the First World War started, which was hardly a good omen; it is said that Shackleton paused off Land's End and telegraphed Churchill to ask if they should cancel the trip and put themselves at the disposal of the War Office. Churchill is reputed to have replied with one word: 'Proceed.' He probably saw a successful expedition as good morale-boosting for Britain.

Proceed they did, as far as the Weddell Sea, and straight into far earlier and thicker pack ice than had been anticipated. The expedition ship, *Endurance*, was crushed and disabled to such an extent that the entire crew had to take to the boats. Crean, the animal-lover, was heartbroken when he had to shoot the puppies of one of their sled dogs, which he had nursed throughout the voyage, as well as the ship's cat. There was no place in the boats for those that served no useful purpose.

From the rocking boats they watched as the ship was inexorably squashed and eventually sank. Now came an incredible 492 days of survival. They first landed on, and then drifted among, the ice floes, before Shackleton decided that they should try to make for Elephant Island in the South Shetlands. Here at least solid ground might be found, even if no people. Many of the crew were suffering the inevitable effects of exhaustion and malnutrition, and by the time they reached a firm beach on the island, it was evident that most of them could go no further. Fortunately, there were seals and penguins to provide food, and they melted ice for water, but conditions were pretty bad, and about to get worse as winter set in.

Nothing for it, decided Shackleton, but to take a small party of six in one lifeboat, the *James Caird*, and try to reach South Georgia, where it was known there were Norwegian whaling stations. Crean was in demand on both sides: those remaining on Elephant Island wanted him to stay and look after them, but Shackleton knew how valuable he would be on the highly dangerous voyage. Crean himself was determined to go – it was always in his nature to set out and find solutions rather than wait for them to come to him. The saying 'don't wait for your ship to come in – swim out to meet it' might have been made with Crean in mind.

It took the little *James Caird* all of sixteen days to reach South Georgia, battling gale-force winds and enormous waves all the way, with bailing a never-ending task. When eventually they did make landfall, it was on the southern side of the island. Here there was nothing, all the whaling stations being on the north side. They had no choice but to undertake a crossing on foot of the totally unexplored mountainous interior.

Only three of that already pitifully small party were even fit enough to undertake this appalling challenge: Shackleton himself, Tom Crean and Worsley. The remaining three stayed on that harsh beach, trying to find some shelter and hoping against hope for their companions' success. There followed a gruelling thirty-seven-hour nonstop trek, steps often having to be bitterly retraced as they reached the top of a crest only to find unnavigable chaos beyond.

At last, they reached Stromness whaling station, more dead than alive, and were able to organise rescue for the men left behind on the south side of the island. It took a lot longer to find a ship willing and capable of the dangerous journey back to Elephant Island and the party left behind there for months, but eventually that was achieved too. There then remained only the rescue of the Ross Sea party, which had been laying food supplies along the line of the original expedition – supplies that would never be needed. The *James Caird*, which made that incredible journey from Elephant Island to South Georgia, is now on display at Shackleton's old school, Dulwich College.

Back in Britain at last, in November 1916, Tom Crean learned not only that the war was still continuing in Europe, as fiercely as ever, but also that his own country had made its bid for freedom in the Easter Rising of that year – at just about the time when he and his crewmates became stranded on Elephant Island. Promoted to the rank of warrant officer in recognition of his service on the recent expedition, he received his third Polar medal to add to the Albert and the two from previous trips.

By now, he must have had enough of horrors and the struggle for survival and yearned for the simpler pleasures of life. In September 1917, he married a girl from his home village, Eileen Herlihy.

When Shackleton, ever-enthusiastic even after his bad experiences, started organising another Antarctic expedition in early 1920, he invited Crean and several others from the *Endurance* to join him, but this time Crean said no. He had a young family now, and was planning to refurbish and open the pub he had bought many years earlier. An injury from a fall on board ship resulted in his retirement from the Navy on medical grounds that same year. Now he and his wife were able to open that pub in Annascaul, which they christened the South Pole Inn.

That is about the only acknowledgement by this otherwise shy and retiring man of the amazingly adventurous existence he had lived up to then. Throughout his life, he refused to talk about those days, tucking away his medals and keeping his own counsel. This could well have been because of the changed political situation in Ireland, with the struggle raging for independence from England. A past, however adventurous, in the English Royal Navy was not something to put on public view by then, although back in the 1870s, it was one of the few options available to the young Kerryman. Crean and his family lived a peaceful life in Annascaul, well-liked by everyone, and if sometimes he went back in dreams to those terrifying days and nights in the Antarctic, he didn't speak about it.

Sad to relate, Tom Crean, who had miraculously escaped death so many times in those adventurous years, fell victim to appendicitis in 1938 and died in the Bon Secours hospital in Cork on 27 July, just days after his sixty-first birthday. He was buried in the plain family tomb that he himself had built in Ballinacourty, not far from Annascaul.

This was a shy and retiring but strong and courageous man, born and bred in the gentle Irish countryside, who travelled further through inhospitable oceans, saw more incredible sights and endured more frightening conditions than most people of his time or indeed ours, but who in the end returned safely home across the sea to his own place and his own people.

Left: Tomb of the Crean family at Ballinacourty. Below: The South Pole Inn, established by Tom Crean and his wife.

The bay on Valentia Island from where the
first transatlantic message was sent.

CHAPTER VIII

Ireland Calling

THE NEWSHOUND, THE INVENTOR
AND THE LONG, LONG CABLE

For millennia, Ireland was at the very edge of the
known world, alone and apart, almost untouched by events
elsewhere. In the nineteenth century, as scientific discover-
ies and technology developed and grew, it was to become the
centre of a new and hitherto undreamed-of network, span-
ning the oceans. Ireland became the bridge over the huge gap
between the old and the new, between Europe and Asia on
the one side and the Americas on the other.

The newshound: Reuter

Julius Reuter was first off the starting blocks. Born in Germany in 1816, he became keenly interested in the experiments

of Gauss, studying the transmission of electrical signals. Starting out in publishing, he moved to Paris in 1848 to work with the news agency Havas, later to become Agence France Presse. Keenly watching the development of telegraphy, Reuter foresaw opportunities in the swift transmission of the very latest news. He soon moved to Aachen, where he set up his own office, using homing pigeons to send messages between there and Brussels, thereby linking the all-important centres of Berlin and Paris.

The pigeon, winging swiftly through the skies, was actually faster than the post train, and thus provided Reuter with the latest news from the financial markets before anybody else. This was valuable information for which his business clients would readily pay, and business prospered. When technology improved sufficiently, the hardworking pigeons were retired from active duty, to be replaced by a direct telegraph link. The man who was to give his name to a worldwide organisation, recognised today as the foremost in its field, was on his way.

Reuter knew instinctively that moving fast was the key to success. As soon as a direct telegraph was established between Europe and England, he moved to London and set up his company near the Stock Exchange there, so as to supply the latest figures to clients on the Continent. But his brain never ceased working, and his eye was already looking further afield – to the New World, and the possibilities of creating a link to the growing world of industry and business there.

By this time, Ireland was connected by telegraph to England – a vital necessity for the controlling Crown powers, who needed to keep an eye on everything in the rebellious island, as well as for merchants and businessmen. And so Julius made his plans. In the early 1860s, he slipped across to Cork, travelled down into the far southwest and found just the right place for his experiments – Crookhaven and Brow Head. Reuter had an overhead telegraph wire constructed all the way from Crookhaven to Cork – no easy matter, when you consider the rough terrain, poor roads and many hills and valleys in between – and set up a station from which to conduct his trials.

Crookhaven had been a well-known harbour for centuries before Reuter's arrival. It was the last port in Ireland before the long journey across the Atlantic, and the first one reached by ships coming eastward. Here they could rest and take on food and water, before continuing their journeys. Lloyds shipping agency had a representative here from at least the eighteenth century, recording the vessels that passed or called in, and sending the information back to head office in London. Now Reuter was going to take things a step further.

Crookhaven has been a busy port for centuries.

In the mid-nineteenth century, letters from America could take two to three weeks or more to arrive in Europe. Mail and despatches for Ireland were dropped off at Cobh (then called Queenstown), while those for England were taken on to Bristol, Liverpool or London, for onward transmission by rail. Central Europe took even longer. Julius Reuter could see how valuable a swifter service would be to government, business and financial markets.

There had been a look-out tower on Brow Head from Napoleonic times, used afterwards by Lloyds and other interested representatives to check shipping. Now Reuter set up new arrangements whereby vessels bound from the New World would drop off canisters with the latest news despatches written by his special correspondents in New York, Boston or any of the major ports in America. His look-outs would spot the approaching mail ship and send a signal down to Crookhaven, so that a small boat could go out to catch the bobbing canister (supplied with a flag and a blue light to enable it to be seen – Julius thought of everything) and bring it ashore.

The news was swiftly assessed and passed along the telegraph wire to Cork, from where it went to London, arriving long before the inbound ship could moor at the docks there. The *Cork Examiner* often boasted that it had the latest news well in advance of England's capital city, since it kept a sharp eye on the telegraph wire from Crookhaven and could get the story on the front page immediately.

The shattering news of Abraham Lincoln's assassination in April 1865 arrived in this way: McLean, the New York Reuter's correspondent, heard it over the wire there, immediately

The Marconi tower and signal station on Brow Head.

scribbled his despatch and rushed down to the docks to send it. The mail ship *Teutonia*, for Hamburg via London, had just sailed, but they bred them tough and resilient at Reuter's. McLean chartered a tugboat and chased the ocean-going vessel until he got close enough to throw his package on board. It was duly dropped off under Brow Head in West Cork, and immediately wired on to Cork and then London. Reuter had got in ahead of the pack and scooped the top story of the century. It became one of the most memorable achievements of the agency, and even featured in a Hollywood film of 1940, *A Dispatch from Reuter's*, with Edward G Robinson as the legendary newsman.

A born newsman, Reuter was one of the first to realise that swift communications were going to become increasingly important, and that clients would pay well for such speed. However, there was still that long sea journey to be factored in.

Boats had certainly increased their speed and the time it took to cross the Atlantic had reduced, but it was still a matter of weeks rather than days. Taking to the skies was an option of course, but carrier pigeons were not inclined to volunteer for the transatlantic route if they could help it, and the age of air travel was still a long way in the future.

This is where an enthusiastic inventor, son of an Irish mother and an Italian father, comes into the story and to the very same location, Crookhaven.

The inventor: Marconi

When young Annie Jameson, of the famous Irish distilling family, went to Italy to study opera singing in the mid-nineteenth century, she little expected to meet her future husband there – but that is exactly what happened. She and widower Guiseppe Marconi, an aristocratic landowner, fell madly in love; however, her family insisted she was far too young, and whisked her home to Daphne Castle in Wexford.

Annie knew her own mind though, and as soon as she was of age, she went back and married her Italian. Guglielmo, the second of their children, and the one destined to make the greatest mark on the world as the father of modern radio communications, was born in 1874.

Keenly interested in the emerging science of radio waves, by the age of twenty he was already conducting experiments at their home in Pontevecchio, often assisted by the family butler as well as his mother, who encouraged him in everything he did. It was she who brought him to England and to Ireland, introduced him to people who could help him achieve his ambitions, and mustered backing for the world's first patent application for a system of telegraphy in 1896. The young Marconi developed portable transmitter and receiver set-ups that could work over long distances, thereby moving from in-house experiments to a real-life communication system.

In 1897, he succeeded in establishing direct links between Britain and the Continent, and set up the Wireless Telegraph and Signal Company. Already, though, his eyes were set on America and the possibility of getting instant communication across the Atlantic. It seemed an impossible challenge, but Marconi was determined, and began to think of the southwest of Ireland as a good place to try. He was, of course, already very familiar with this country through his mother, and indeed in 1904 married Beatrice O'Brien, daughter of the 14th Baron Inchiquin (they divorced by mutual agreement some years later).

Having set up a signal station at Poldhu in Cornwall, he now did the same at Brow Head. This was an ideal site, 100 metres above sea level and with no obstruction between it and the next landfall to the west, America. With Reuter and Lloyds already using the location for ship to shore signals, it was clearly the right place to be.

After much trial and failure, Marconi succeeded in establishing a link between Poldhu and Brow Head, which proved what he had suspected: that wireless signals don't travel in straight lines, but follow the Earth's natural curve. That was all he needed to push on with his goal of making contact with North America. This was finally achieved in December 1901,

Arthur 'Daddy' Nottage, always happy to swap stories of the old days in his Crookhaven pub.

when Brow Head and St John's, Newfoundland, were finally linked by radio signal. The following year, Marconi set up a telegraphic station in Crookhaven and brought six experienced wireless operators across from England. One of these was Arthur Nottage, a former Morse code operator on the London and North Eastern railway.

Nottage settled happily into his work at Brow Head, being paid £1 a week and lodging in Crookhaven village. He met and married a local woman, Hannah Notter, and when in 1914 Marconi moved the station to Valentia Island, Nottage chose to stay on and run the Welcome Inn, which still stands today. 'Daddy Nottage', as he was affectionately known, was a central figure in the culture of Crookhaven, loved by locals and visitors alike, until his death in 1974 broke the direct link between the present day and Guglielmo Marconi.

The role played by the Marconi system in sea rescues did much to raise public awareness of the value of radio and brought its indefatigable founder into the public eye. This was particularly so in two great maritime disasters, those of the *Titanic* in 1912 and the *Lusitania* in 1915. Two Marconi radio operators, Jack Phillips and Harold Bride, were on board the *Titanic* when it struck that iceberg, and immediately sent SOS signals. The *Carpathia*, some fifty-eight miles away, got the distress calls very quickly and instantly went to the rescue, picking up many survivors. Of the two radio operators, only Bride survived the sinking.

There is a strange addendum to that story: Marconi himself had been offered free passage on the *Titanic* on its maiden (and, as it turned out, its only) voyage, but had chosen to take the *Lusitania* instead, because he thought the secretarial facilities were better on the latter.

Robert Leith was the Marconi radio operator aboard the *Lusitania* on the ship's final voyage. When the ship was torpedoed on 7 May 1915, off the Old Head of Kinsale, Leith and his assistant radio operator, David McCormick, continued to radio constantly for help. They only abandoned their posts near the end when water was lapping the boat deck, and went instead to the rescue of as many passengers as they could. Both were among the survivors who came ashore at Cobh. Again, it was thanks to Marconi's invention that so many did survive, though such a huge number were lost. The Nobel Prize he was awarded in 1909 was well deserved.

The long, long cable: Ireland and North America

Ireland's key role in the final establishment of strong and effective communication between the Old and New Worlds came in 1866 when the mammoth – many said impossible – challenge of laying a continuous cable across the Atlantic Ocean bed was successfully met. It had been thought of for over two decades, but was a staggering project even to consider, let alone put into operation.

In the first place, the cable would have to be of a strength and durability to survive the terrible rigours of such deep waters. It would also need to be of such an incredible length that it would require an enormous ship, of a kind that didn't

The transatlantic cable being hauled ashore in Newfoundland, 1866. Painting by Robert Charles Dudley.

yet exist, to carry its supremely heavy coils during the laying procedure. Despite these challenges, work went ahead. Economies on both sides of the ocean were booming, and the benefits of that communication cable would be huge.

By early 1857, work had started on manufacturing the cable. In August of that year, two ships, one American and one British, started to lay it, heading out from Valentia Island. After 380 miles, the cable snapped. There was nothing to do but return to port. Another 700 miles of cable was made (and creating every inch of that massive cord was a huge exercise in engineering).

For the second attempt, the two ships came from opposite sides and met in mid-Atlantic, where the ends were spliced together. They broke. They were re-spliced, and laying from that central point began. After forty miles, the cable broke again. And again at 146 miles.

But the determined minds behind the scheme wouldn't give up. There was enough cable left for one more attempt. And a year after that first try, Valentia in Ireland and Trinity Bay in Newfoundland were linked by cable. Success!

Well, for a while anyway. On 16 August 1858, the message 'Glory to God in the highest, and on Earth peace, goodwill to men' was transmitted. Unfortunately, the engineer in charge applied too high a voltage and this damaged the cable, which stopped working after three weeks. They must have felt like going back to carrier pigeons.

Seven years went by before another attempt was made. This time they used a really huge ship, the *Great Eastern*, the largest one of its kind at the time. She managed to lay 1,200 miles before the inevitable happened and the cable snapped. Efforts were made to find the broken end on the floor of the Atlantic, but to no avail.

The men behind the project do deserve some praise for their doggedness, which in the end won them the prize they had sought for so long. On 27 July 1866, that incredible feat of manufacturing, the Transatlantic Cable, was hauled ashore in Newfoundland, 1,686 nautical miles from Valentia. Queen Victoria sent a congratulatory message to the American President over the cable, and it was open for business.

Only for the well-to-do businessman, though: it cost $1 per *letter*, not per word, to send a message in those early days of speedy transatlantic correspondence. But for the few who could and did use it, the benefits were enormous. We take instant communication for granted today; back then it was a miracle. And on little Valentia Island, off the Kerry coast, a whole new industry came into being, servicing this latest and greatest international link. In 1966, the cable station finally closed, yielding to more modern technology and newer, stronger cables elsewhere (although the marine radio station, set up here in 1914, continues to supply a vital service to shipping). Visitors, however, come from far and wide to Valentia, as indeed to Crookhaven, to explore their history, and to relive those glory days when Ireland and its surrounding seas were at the very centre of world communication.

The marine radio station on Valentia Island supplies a vital service to shipping.

Other books by Jo Kerrigan and Richard Mills

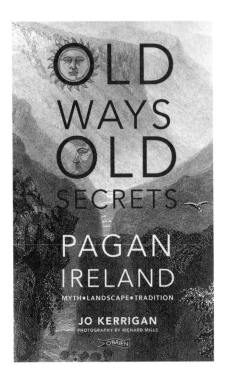

Today's Ireland has never lost the link with its pagan past, never forgotten the old ways. This book reveals the hidden world of pagan Ireland, showing it still exists among the people and in the landscape where it belongs.

ISBN: 9781847172815

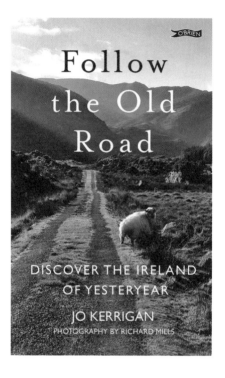

Follow
the Old
Road

DISCOVER THE IRELAND
OF YESTERYEAR

JO KERRIGAN
PHOTOGRAPHY BY RICHARD MILLS

By turning off the main highway and discovering old
routes, some of which have been travelled for thousands of years, you will see Ireland in an entirely
different way. Follow the Old Road will take you
on a tour of a variety of pathways from great river
roads to lost railways.

ISBN: 9781847179111

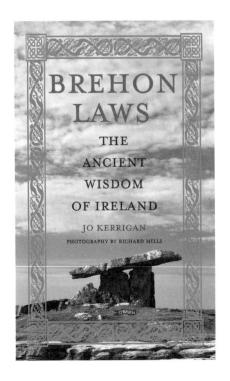

BREHON
LAWS
THE
ANCIENT
WISDOM
OF IRELAND

JO KERRIGAN
PHOTOGRAPHY BY RICHARD MILLS

Celtic Ireland was a land of tribes and warriors;
but a sophisticated & enlightened legal system was
widely accepted. The brehons were the keepers
of these laws, which dealt with every aspect of life:
land disputes; theft or violence; marriage & divorce;
the care of trees & animals.

ISBN: 9781788491075

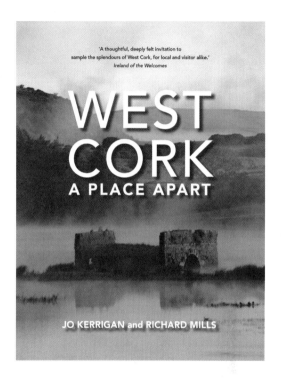

'A thoughtful, deeply felt invitation to sample the splendours of West Cork, for local and visitor alike.'
Ireland of the Welcomes

WEST CORK
A PLACE APART

JO KERRIGAN and RICHARD MILLS

Welcome to the spirit, moods and amazing views of the wonderful world of West Cork, truly a place apart. From the well-known highlights to byways off the beaten track, this enchanting book is for local and visitor alike.

ISBN: 9781847178886